Professional Development Series....
Current Themes in Gifted Education
Elinor Katz, Editor

Teens With Talent

Developing the Potential of the Bright, Brighter and Brightest

Ellie Schatz and Nancy Schuster

pen Space Communications, Inc.

Library of Congress Cataloging-in-Publication Data
Schatz, Ellie.
  Teens with talent: developing the potential of the bright, brighter and brightest/Ellie Schatz, Nancy Schuster; edited by Elinor Katz.
        p. cm. — (Professional development series — current themes in gifted education)
  Includes bibliographical references (p.).
  ISBN 0-9638228-8-8
  1. Gifted teenagers—Education—United States. 2. Achiever motivation in adolescence—United States. 3. Educational acceleration—United States. 4. Gifted teenagers—United State Case studies. I. Schuster, Nancy. II. Katz, Elinor. III. Ti IV. Series.
LC3993.9.S38 1996
371.95'6—dc20   96-8164
                                              CIP

Printed in the United States of America
10 9 8 7 6 5 4 3 2 1

pen Space Communications, Inc.
1900 Folsom, Suite 108
Boulder, CO 80302
(303)444-7020/FAX(303)545-6505

> ## *DEDICATION*
>
> *With appreciation and love to Alex,*
>
> *Chris, Glen, Deena and all the youth*
>
> *whose talents have opened our minds*
>
> *and touched our hearts.*

ACKNOWLEDGMENTS

• Thanks to Paul and Tony for their encouragement, support and practical advice
• To Bob, Julie and Kristin who reviewed the manuscript and provided thoughtful suggestions
• To all the students and parents who shared their ideas and experiences with us
• And to the staff and Board of Directors of the Wisconsin Center for Academically Talented Youth, our families, and friends for having faith in the process and the product.

CONTENTS

Foreword by Karen B. Rogers

Preface

FOREWORD

Authors Ellie Schatz and Nancy Schuster tell us in their preface that they have written this book because of the disturbing decline in achievement among high ability learners in this country. Although much of the blame for this decline can be attributed to school systems that currently place most of their limited resources and efforts on bringing up the achievement of those who have difficulty learning, some of the blame must be placed on gifted educators themselves.

In the past five years more and more discussion in our field has been concerned with replacing *gifted* education with *talent development* education. On the surface there should be nothing wrong with that, provided gifted educators are defining "talent" similarly. But instead of defining talent as extraordinary performance (and therefore requiring extraordinary measures for its development), many in the field are using talent to describe any strength, no matter what its power or amount, as "talent." Thus, in feeding into the general education system, gifted educators are trying to "educate" or enrich almost every child in our schools.

I respect altruism, but when one looks at the history of this field, with its inconsistent philosophical and financial support, I don't think we can afford to be all that altruistic. If gifted educators don't stand up for the gifted and talented, it is a sure bet that no one else in educational circles will.

Teens With Talent: Developing the Potential of the Bright, Brighter and Brightest presents the facts of our current situation in gifted education. It takes a no-nonsense approach to identifying talent through out-of level achievement testing and confronts the issue of *excellence vs equity* head-on. It points out the limitations of classroom teachers and schools in providing the differentiated educational programming gifted and talented children need for full development of their potential. It also hits hard on parents' responsibilities to pick up where the school leaves off—that is, to provide out-of school learning opportunities, home responsibilities and community service experiences.

But this book is more than just confrontive or factual in nature; it specifies clearly and practically what parents can do, how they can make decisions they can live with for their talented teen and comprehensively lists options from which parents may choose. It does these things giving concrete examples of real live kids, without resorting to educational jargon or arcane research studies. It is a book for both lay and professional, but its research underpinnings are powerful. In my own syntheses of research on differentiated programming strategies, the options both inside and out of school, which these authors describe and recommend, are fully supported.

This book may become, and deserves to be, "Dr. Spock" for raising talented teenagers! I sure wish it had been around when our family was making our "best" decisions for our own children.

Karen B. Rogers
University of St. Thomas
St. Paul, Minnesota

PREFACE

Dear Readers:
National statistics suggest that our bright students are not
measuring up to their counterparts from around the world.
Who cares that these students are not working to their potential? We believe that many parents and educators certainly do
care and that there is a way American education can better
address the talented child's needs.

Do you think your child might be above average? If so, what
does that mean? Are you satisfied with his education? Do you
believe that he is measuring up to his full potential? Do you
wonder if you should be doing something more or different to
develop a special talent or interest he might have? Do you
think your school should be doing something more or different? Do you feel as if you are alone in asking questions like
these? Is your child moving into the preteen or teenage years
with your questions of talent development looming larger than
ever?

We have written *Teens With Talent: Developing the Potential
of the Bright, Brighter and Brightest* for parents and educators
because for them the above are real questions. We have written this book because of the very disturbing decline in the
achievement of high-ability children in this country. Through
the telling of personal stories, we can help answer these questions, address this decline and offer help to those embarking on
a talent development quest.

Parents of bright children have always been plagued by the
misconception that a bright or talented child will make it on his
own. Added to this traditional myth are new ones, including
questions of gender and the current rampant opinion that tests
are bad. We have written this book because misconceptions
and myths prevail about bright, talented and gifted children and
what they need. Because parents and colleagues have asked us
to share our more than 30 combined years of experience in
gifted education, we have written *Teens With Talent*.

If any of the above issues, ideas or questions strike the slightest
chord with you, this book can help. Some parents of bright
children take a research approach to finding answers to their

questions of talent development, and if you are among this group, you probably feel a need to read just about everything. This book can provide a beginning or add fuel to the fire you already have going. Other parents rely on school personnel and/or private consultants to provide most of the answers to their questions. If you find yourself in this category, this book can help you determine which paths you wish to explore with the professionals by making you more effective in approaching them with some background and direction. Still other parents internalize their questions and the myths they hear, often resulting in varying degrees of frustration, guilt, anger and blame. If you see yourself in this category, *Teens With Talent* will address some of your questions and trigger new ones, let you know that you are not alone and set you on a path of positive inquiry.

If you are the parent or teacher of a bright child between the ages of 10 and 17, and you have on one or more occasions wished someone would tell you what to do, you should read this book. In fact, if your child is 6, 7 or 8, you might want to plan now for options in the coming preteen and teen years. A parent, who took the research approach to his children's talent development in the early 80s, recently noted with dismay that parents are asking the same questions today that he asked over a decade ago. He states that in spite of all the information out there, "They still need a concise, lucid, experientially-based publication." This is that publication.

Ellie Schatz and Nancy Schuster
May, 1996

The letter above directly addresses parents, and throughout the entire book we continue to do so. But, we wish to state emphatically that this book is intended for educators as well. If you are a resource teacher for the gifted, a gifted-program coordinator, a counselor or another person charged with providing modified curriculum and classes or finding options that match the needs of talented children, this book can help you guide your bright students into appropriate programming options.

1- Indicators of Talent

Just as there is no magic formula for bringing up children, there is no clear-cut indicator of future intellectual eminence when a child is born. As parents, you cannot help but pay attention as your child grows, and if along the way you wonder what it means if your child is bright, you are not alone.

When pressed for what he thought his greatest ability was, one child said, "It's not only that I catch on fast, it's also that I ask a lot of questions. Maybe too many questions." Is this child bright? If, in similar ways, you often find yourself wondering about the nature of your own child's responses and actions, most likely it is because you have noticed natural and real indicators of talent, which may be advanced vocabulary, curiosity, intensity or extreme sensitivity. If this is so, then what you more than likely need is threefold: confirmation of your observations, a measure of how bright she is compared to other bright children, and assurances that you or others will be able to help her become all she is capable of becoming.

Although we should all feel safe talking about characteristics of learning that indicate special abilities or interests in children, such discussions are difficult for many educators. Regular classroom teachers often have little training in the field of gifted education and consequently are afraid of labeling children. They sometimes feel that any mention of special talents will hurt other youngsters who may be less talented. They are stuck with a paradox — school missions explicitly state that individual learning needs of all students must be met, yet the political climate of many schools makes it difficult to talk about individual differences and educational implications. Leaders in the field of gifted education believe deeply that schools can and must implement strategies that will meet the specific learning needs of bright children, and they believe that identification is not about labeling. They know that characteristics of giftedness need to be measured and understood because this knowledge suggests different actions which parents and schools must consider in order to ensure optimal academic, social and emotional development of their children.

As a parent or educator with this book in hand, you have the broad psychological support of thousands of educators nation-wide who are comfortable with questions about talent development. Take a moment now to envision these thousands crowded around you for support as we explore your thoughts and concerns.

Identification — Definitions and Attitudes

One student is bright. Another student is brighter. A third is the brightest. What does all this mean? Different approaches can be used to answer questions of identification. In this section we will first examine the historical approach of using intelligence test data, then go on to examine newer approaches such as standardized test score analysis, consideration of multiple intelligences (Gardner, 1983) or reliance on a combination of objective and subjective data.

In the early decades of this century, a question regarding degree of brightness would probably have been viewed as a legitimate and measurable inquiry about giftedness or general intelligence. A school might have administered group intelligence tests in the classrooms or the school psychologist might have used an individual intelligence test, such as the Stanford-Binet, to determine a child's mental age compared to his chronological age. An intelligence quotient (IQ) of 100 indicated an average score. An IQ of approximately 125 or above often was defined as gifted for the purpose of placing children in gifted programs.

Using this definition now, if your child has an IQ of about 125, you are right to think of her as bright. If your child has an IQ of about 145, obviously she is brighter, meaning there is an even greater difference between her mental age and her chronological age. If her IQ is measured at 160 or above, the greater the discrepancy is between her mental and chronological age, along with the increased chance that someone will confirm your instincts that she is among the brightest.

A problem with this historical definition is that it is out of favor in the schools, which reflects the climate of our communities at large. Our society, in its efforts to provide equal opportunity for all, has fallen into the trap of equal treatment of all. A statement attributed to Thomas Jefferson holds that nothing is as unequal as the equal treatment of unequals. If use of IQ legitimately communicates a kind of inequality of intellectual abilities between people, then equal treatment of them in the schools suggests existence of a problem to be tackled. Unequals are being treated as if they were the same, and that is a touchy issue. What is being asked is that schools distinguish between equal opportunity and equal treatment, and if society cannot do that, how can we expect the schools to act otherwise?

Suppose you do not care about societal attitudes; you decide that if an IQ score will answer your questions, you want to have your child's IQ measured. Do not ask about group IQ tests. They are rarely, if ever, used today, and for good reason. Their effectiveness and accuracy in measuring what they were supposed to measure was found to be lacking. Individual IQ tests, however, are deemed by psychologists to be reliable and valid for measuring general intelligence. However, they are also used less often today by the schools, and unless your child is having extreme problems with learning or behavior it is unlikely that your school personnel will feel that your request merits the time and cost of such individual attention. If you want this kind of data to answer your questions, you may have to rely on a private testing service. Colleges and universities often have testing clinics with minimal fees attached, so if money is a factor you might start by calling there.

Getting an IQ score will confirm, or sometimes fail to confirm, your observations by putting your child's intellectual abilities on a numerical scale. But it might not help you with the third part of your inquiry: how to help her become all that she is capable of being. Educators who do not accept the idea of intellectual differences will probably be unimpressed with an IQ in the 125-130 range. They will most likely not deny that your child is bright, but they may suggest that many other children with lower IQs or for whom IQs are unknown are equally bright or able. IQ, they will often say, is simply not a fair measure of potential. This is because many educators assume average performance in the classroom means average ability. They are unaware of the stultifying effect of the average classroom on highly capable students.

However, a school psychologist, principal, or teacher is apt to be more impressed with a very high IQ. This is not because they will necessarily like the idea of inequality between your child and another, but because they recognize that something out of the ordinary should be done. The problem, which we will address later, is what should be done.

Linda Silverman (1993) states, "Despite various concerns about intelligence testing, the intelligence quotient does provide valuable information about the rate at which cognitive development outstrips physical development and therefore is an index of the degree of asynchrony" (p. 4). The term *asynchrony*, which suggests that gifted children are intellectually out of sync or without a peer group, may be useful to you. One reason many parents begin asking these kinds of questions concerning intellect is that they feel their child is out of sync. Peer groups for adults are frequently defined by what they do and who shares their interests. Peer groups for children are most often defined by chronological age because that is how they are grouped in school. Adults have the freedom to seek a true peer group. Children do not.

So it follows that the higher a child's IQ, the greater the degree of intellectual asynchrony and the less apt educators will be to dismiss it. In other words, if your child was found to have an IQ of 135 when she was 6, her mental age was 8. Most schools consider a difference that small to be something they can handle without pointing it out or labeling the child. Keep in mind, though, that one of the reasons you may be getting increasingly frustrated as your child ages is that the discrepancy between mental and chronological age increases as she gets older. If your daughter is now 12 (still with an IQ of 135), her mental age is now 16, and she is four (rather than two) years out of sync with normal school progression.

Suppose your daughter was found to have an IQ of 170 when she was 6. Her mental age was then 10 1/2. If she is now age 12, her mental age is 20 (Silverman, p. 5). Because she was clearly much out of sync when she was very little, the chances are that the schools did intervene in some way. The incongruity between her cognitive development and her physical development was probably easy to see. Differences in rate of development, however, are more than just between the physical and mental. A child may also be socially and emotionally out of sync. Society does not relate well to a 12 year old who responds like a 20 year old. This creates an inner tension that could be mirrored by outer adjustment problems.

Today, when you approach schools with questions about intelligence, they may say they focus on children's talents instead of giftedness. In the past two decades it has not been uncommon for educators to dismiss the g word, or at least not start with it. Lower case g now has two connotations, and both are considered negative by many educators. Such educators fear: (1) g means general intelligence (the original meaning) and this is bad because schools are supposed to be democratic, educating everyone equally as we mentioned, and not producing a cognitive elite; and (2) g means gifted which is bad because it labels children. Those who are labeled gifted might feel superior and those who are not labeled gifted might feel inferior.

Two more recent approaches to addressing these questions were popular in schools across the country in the 1970s to 1980s. First, the federal government, in an attempt to broaden the definition of giftedness, legislated the following definition:

Gifted and talented children are those identified by professionally qualified persons, who by virtue of outstanding abilities are capable of high performance. These are children... with demonstrated achievement and/or potential in any of the following areas, singly or in combination: (a) general intellectual ability; (b) specific academic aptitude; (c) creative or productive thinking; (d) leadership ability; (e) visual and performing arts ability; and (f) psychomotor ability (Marland, 1972, p. 2).

The federal definition did not differentiate between talented and gifted. You will also notice that it makes the categories appear to be parallel, when in fact they are interrelated. For instance, creative ability and leadership ability should not occur alongside academic, artistic or athletic abilities; they occur within and across them. This definition did accomplish the goal of expanding perceptions of giftedness and is still in use in many states today as their legislated definition of giftedness.

A second definition popular with schools was based on studies of creative-productive adults by Joseph Renzulli (1978). Renzulli's research showed that three traits identify persons who achieve recognition for their unique accomplishments and creative contributions. These traits, known as the three-ring conception of giftedness, or the Renzulli definition, are above-average ability, creativity and task-commitment. This definition introduced characteristics of motivation into the gifted framework and further suggested that giftedness was achieved over time.

In 1985, the idea of perceiving potential from the standpoint of talent was advanced by Benjamin Bloom. He defined talent as a demonstrated ability, achievement or skill in a specific field of study or interest. Specific abilities, such as a talent for drawing, mathematics, swimming or piano playing, could easily be observed, nurtured and developed — or could just as easily be ignored, neglected and lost due to environmental conditions. Use of a talent development approach in the schools was predicated on the belief that human beings have the capacity for multiple talents, that many or all children come to school with some special talent, and that because there are so many individual talents everyone should have a talent niche within which to feel good.

Although the vestiges of the federal definition remain in many schools, and talent is thus delineated into five categories for the purposes of determining services (intellectual, creative, artistic, leadership and specific academic), a newer talent development framework is fast becoming popular. Howard Gardner (1983) has advanced the theory of multiple intelligences. He states:

Multiple intelligence theory posits a small set of human intellectual potentials, perhaps as few as seven in number, of which all individuals are capable by virtue of their membership in the human species. Owing

*to heredity, early training, or, in all probability, a constant interaction
between these factors, some individuals will develop certain intelligences
far more than others; but every normal individual should develop each
intelligence to some extent, given but a modest opportunity to do so* (p.
278).

According to this framework, then, as summarized by Thomas
Armstrong (1994), a person may be identified as having some
ability or exceptional abilities in one or more of the following
seven areas:

- *linguistic — the capacity to use words effectively*
- *logical-mathematical — the capacity to use numbers
  effectively and to reason well*
- *spatial — the ability to perceive the visual-spatial world
  accurately and to perform transformations upon those
  perceptions*
- *bodily-kinesthetic — expertise in using one's whole body
  to express ideas and feelings and facility in using one's
  hands to produce or transform things*
- *musical — the capacity to perceive, discriminate,
  transform, and express musical forms*
- *interpersonal — the ability to perceive and make
  distinctions in the moods, intentions, motivations, and
  feelings of other people*
- *intrapersonal — self-knowledge and the ability to act
  adaptively on the basis of that knowledge* (pp. 2-3).

Asked why he called them intelligences and not talents or
abilities, Gardner explained, "If I'd said that there's [sic] seven
kinds of competencies, people would yawn and say 'Yeah, yeah.'
But by calling them 'intelligences,' I'm saying that we've tended to
put on a pedestal one variety called intelligence, and there's
actually a plurality of them, and some are things we've never
thought about as being 'intelligence' at all" (Armstrong, p. 4).

The gradual movement from the 1970s through the 1990s
toward broadening the definition of giftedness has led to the
identification first of more children as gifted or talented and now
to all children as fitting somewhere in the talent or high-intelli-
gence framework. We like the idea of leaving open the possibilities for extraordinary human achievement rather than closing
doors through an early and narrow identification process. However, the multiple intelligences idea raises several new cautions as
it is interpreted and applied by the schools. Are all children being
forced to fit into one of the seven categories? If so, the framework
no longer helps us to understand giftedness. Are the schools
using the seven categories to identify children or to better define
programming techniques that match their various learning styles?

The latter is fine, but the framework is then no longer a tool for defining or understanding high intelligence.

Talent Indicators at School

The previous definitions of intelligence and talents are tools for understanding your child's learning needs. Schools use more tools such as tests, portfolios and report cards. These provide feedback on how your child is achieving against some measure of expectation of how she should or could be achieving. The feedback may be objective, subjective or some combination of the two; it may compare the child with other children or against herself.

A common indicator of talent in school has always been the report card. Whether students receive letter grades, rankings on a predetermined scale or open-ended teacher comments related to classroom accomplishments and deportment, parents rely on written feedback to tell them how their child is doing. If your child's talent potential exactly matches her talent output, which also exactly matches the teacher's perception of her output, this method will be very satisfying to you. However, this is rarely the case. If you think your child could be challenged more, regardless of how good a report she gets, you will question the accuracy of what is being measured.

An important school indicator of academic talent has always been scores or percentile rankings on standardized tests. Whatever testing battery your school district uses, for example the California Achievement Tests (CAT) or the Iowa Tests of Basic Skills (ITBS), you can easily tell how your child compares in a specific subject with other children from across the country. A 9th stanine or 99th percentile ranking indicates that she is at the top, or scoring better than 99 out of 100 children at the same age and grade level. This information can then be used by the school to form learning groups or determine more critical questions of advancement or retention in a curriculum area or at a grade level.

Today, some schools are trying alternative assessment procedures such as performance- or portfolio-based assessment. Whatever the method used, parents concerned about their child's intellectual abilities and corresponding degree of achievement in school must ask three basic questions:

1. Does the school have an accurate measure of our child's potential to learn difficult material?

2. Is our child learning new material?

3. Do the assessment procedures used by the school document both what our child has accomplished to date and what she needs to learn next?

Misconceptions

Misconceptions about tests and measurements abound. We will examine three that could have an impact on your child's talent development.

1. Misconception: *Standardized achievement tests are bad.* A prevailing school attitude in the 1990s is that achievement tests are harmful to individual children and should therefore be eliminated. In fact, it is not the tests themselves that are bad; rather, it is the misinterpretation and misuse of the data they provide. If used appropriately, one way you can be sure that your bright child is doing well is to refer to standardized test data. It is legitimate for you to expect the schools to provide you with clear indicators of how much your child knows and how this affects what she should be learning.

2. Misconception: *A 95th to 99th percentile ranking on a standardized test means my child is the brightest.* If your student is scoring better than 95 to 99 out of 100 students, she is obviously at the top of something. The question is, "What is that something?" Perhaps such a score does indicate the brightest child, but this cannot be confirmed by that one score. Standardized tests are meant to help schools evaluate how they are teaching, and are geared to measure the average student's achievement. Bright students' similar scores tend to make them appear bunched up at the top of the scale, not showing the variances of their aptitudes beyond the test measurements. This is called the *ceiling effect*, and comes into play when evaluating grade-level standardized test scores for the bright students. It means that potential beyond average grade level has been indicated, but not measured with accuracy. You still only know that your child is bright, but not how bright. If you want to know how much your child is capable of learning beyond typical grade-level expectations, more data is necessary.

3. Misconception: *Students at the top of any indicator of talent do not need to spend time learning skills.* Americans tend to assume that their best students can compete with the best students anywhere. Americans also tend to think that talent indicators are synonymous with skill. Neither is true. International comparisons show that our best students are not receiving an education comparable to that of selected students in other nations. They may be bright or even brightest according to an intelligence test or other measure of potential, but on skill-based measures of achievement in history, science, math, reading etc., as reported by the National Assessment of Educational Progress (NAEP), American students do not measure up (O'Connell Ross, 1993). Bright students must learn basic study and research skills as well as advanced skills in specific fields of knowledge. Only through continuous skill development will they be able to advance their learning. If your child is going to compete in the world community, more than high indicators of talent will be required.

Gathering More Data

Talent Search is a national testing program for middle school students who have previously scored in the 95th percentile (in some regions, 97th percentile) or above on standardized achievement tests. The Scholastic Assessment Test (SAT) or the American College Test (ACT), typically taken by college-bound juniors and seniors, are used. These more difficult tests are said to be out-of-level in this scenario because they are given to students earlier than originally intended. The tests discern variances in the aptitudes of the bright younger students and indicate differences in their individual learning needs. For instance, a student scoring in the 95th percentile on the grade-level standardized test might score in the 90-99th percentile on the out-of-level test. This confirms that she not only understands the typical grade-level material well, but also shows that she has the capacity to reason and conceptualize well beyond grade level. Need for a more rigorous and faster-paced curriculum is indicated. Another student in the 99th percentile on the standardized-achievement test might score in the lower percentiles on the out-of-level test. This means that she has mastered grade level material well at the current pace of instruction. Need for a more accelerated curriculum is not indicated, but enrichment is appropriate.

Talent Search information can be especially critical for two types of bright students. First, it can help exceptionally talented students who seem to be achieving well compared to their classmates, but who are actually years beyond in content and concept mastery. These brightest students are often languishing from a lack of mental stimulation and challenge. Talent Search scores emphasize the need for more advanced or rigorous curriculum. Second, it is important for talented underachievers who, because of their poor school performance, are not seen as bright. These truly bright students are often held back or slowed down, when instead they should be challenged through higher performance expectations. Often high Talent Search scores are a surprise to them and their parents and provide the impetus for entry into more challenging courses.

Some parents reading this may wonder about getting their child involved in Talent Search. "What if my child doesn't score as high as a college-bound senior? Even if many students do score that high every year, it's still pretty hard to do!" The out-of-level testing experience need not be negative for students who score in the lower range of possibilities; all students who have qualified for Talent Search are known to be bright. Here we are using another tool to look for the bright, brighter and brightest. With proper counseling from their parents and/or teachers before taking an out-of-level test, they will know that any score is acceptable and that, bright as they are, there are many skills to be learned as they proceed through school. Good self-esteem is built through positive reinforcement of their courage in taking a test designed for students who are older and have had more years of schooling. Poor scores on these rigorous tests can also indicate a lack of experience with real challenges, a bad reaction to the stress of the test or other non-talent related indicators. One parent who has been through the process suggests, "The social stigma in having younger children take college entrance exams is larger in parents' minds than warranted. You need to understand that this is not a labeling process that will narrow your child's opportunities. Rather, it's a screening that introduces resources and programs that you and your child might otherwise never hear about."

The Talent Search concept can be applied by using other performance assessments. The idea is to administer a valid and reliable measure of achievement beyond what is usually expected of a child that age. Having an art portfolio judged to be exceptional according to established professional criteria or earning a prestigious musical audition at a young age are similar examples of out-of-level assessment. Using out-of-level assessments of any kind that have predictive validity within a given field, teachers and parents can plan for appropriate programming options.

Julian Stanley (1984), founder of the Talent Search method of identification, states, "Diagnostic testing, followed by prescribed instruction, can work wonders. Ascertain what the talented student does not yet know about the subject and help him/her learn just that directly without having to wade through the parts already known." With regard to our concern for assessing g versus developing broader indicators of talent, he adds, "We have a great responsibility to be worthy of the bright and brilliant students with whom we deal...Perhaps by 2001 A.D...we shall have broken the stranglehold of the IQ on our thinking and practice. Of course, one need not throw out the beautiful baby with the dirty bath water. Let's keep what's best about the...concept of general intelligence but supplement it appropriately" (p.179).

Whether you use the Talent Search concept or another means of obtaining more data regarding your child's specific talent potential, the information gathered should be used in educational planning. You are looking for a curriculum that matches your child's specific learning needs. This curriculum might be organized around three guiding principles (Kaplan, 1974):

Content: what is taught; disciplines, issues, problems and themes

Process: how it is applied; basic, research, thinking and problem-solving skills

Product: ways in which learning is communicated

With these principles in mind, you can respond to talent indicators by asking questions that will direct the planning process. For example, you might ask, "If my 7th grader is scoring above average for college-bound seniors on a test of mathematical reasoning, is 7th-grade math, prealgebra or even Algebra I appropriate?" Perhaps an algebra test should be administered to reveal specific mathematical learning needs. Or you might ask, "Even though my 6th-grader is scoring above the mean for college-bound seniors on a test of mathematical reasoning, what mathematical skills hasn't she mastered?" Further diagnostic testing followed by prescribed instruction is indicated. Keep in mind that these youngsters can master very difficult content and that they can grasp new processes at an extremely rapid pace. Their final products should indicate the depth, breadth and quality of their learning.

2-School Is Not Enough

Responding to Talent Indicators — The Problem

In her classic text on gifted education, *Growing Up Gifted*, Barbara Clark (1992) suggests that we have limited what children learn by our notion that there is a limit to what they can learn. Unfortunately, this has become a truism in American schools today. Our children are exposed to easier textbooks, easier curricula and a slower pace at which new ideas are presented than either their parents or grandparents experienced. The problem is paradoxical when coupled with the prevailing "Lake Wobegon Effect," which reflects the general attitude that all children in our schools or communities are above average. This would imply that the scholastic content should be getting harder. No wonder you are confused as to whether school is enough for your talented child when the prevailing educational winds blow him a mild curriculum. Considered temperate enough to make all the children comfortable, such a curriculum will not be hot enough either in content or process to challenge our bright, brighter and brightest learners.

Your responses to some of the common myths or misconceptions about gifted children in school may be indicators of how your child's school perceives talent. Your subsequent understandings may then help you to approach your school with specific concerns regarding content, process and product in any subject area.

1. *Myth: He <u>and</u> she will make it on their own.* Because schools have stated missions to meet the individual learning needs of all children, no group of children should be expected to make it on its own. The schools are legally responsible to teach *every* child something new. In fact, the presumption is that each student will advance one year beyond where he was at the beginning of a given school year. For example, if your son is entering 7th grade and has mastered all the prealgebra mathematics concepts and skills, he has a right to learn something new. Algebra? You have a right to expect algebra, geometry or whatever curriculum is beyond general mathematics. If your son is entering 9th grade and has mastered all the basic grammatical skills of writing as well as having read, comprehended and remembered great works of literature, he has a right to more than a basic freshman writing or literature curriculum. He has a right to advance in his writing and reading skills.

What about your daughter? Unfortunately, parents are often as guilty as educators of making the even greater assumption that girls will make it on their own. We fall into the trap of thinking that girls will listen and do well without special intervention, that girls do not need extra or advanced courses and that they do not need special learning activities, especially if the family budget will be strained. Most of us would not admit to slighting our girls, but research shows that boys are favored when decisions about advancement are made (American Association of University Women, 1991). Parents must actively fight for equal opportunities for their bright girls. Your daughter has as much right to advanced mathematics, literature, writing and science classes as do boys.

2. Myth: Students will not remember material learned at a faster than normal pace. As we mentioned earlier, the normal rate of academic speed in American schools might be likened to a snail's pace when compared to that of learning in other countries. All our children should be moving at a faster pace, and schools are clearly not meeting the individual needs of our bright children if they prevent them from learning new material. Remembering is a function of mastery plus use. More than 20 years of research through Talent Search programs has demonstrated that bright students master material at a very rapid pace. It is the responsibility of the schools to advance students to the next level once they have mastered the content and processes of a given subject to a specified level of knowledge and understanding. If the students never build upon their knowledge or use it again, they may very well lose it through no fault of their own. However, if students do forge ahead via curricular flexibility and implementation of in-school and out-of-school experiences (Stanley, 1991), they will retain their earlier and more basic understandings.

3. Myth: A single program can be developed to meet the needs of all the bright, talented or gifted students in a school. To have the same program for children who are different in degrees and kinds of talent is like having a standard size shoe for all children. We know that if shoes are too small, they cut off circulation to the foot, cause pain and do not allow for growth. In fact, the child will avoid walking and will certainly give up running. Likewise, a program or curriculum that is too small for the child will cut off circulation to the brain, cause pain and not allow for growth. In fact, the child will avoid thinking and give up running through great ideas.

We know that sometimes children have fun playing around

with big shoes. Toddlers, especially, like to imagine what it would be like to wear mommy's or daddy's shoes. But have you ever seen a toddler don big shoes if he was serious about getting someplace? A shoe must fit if the child is going to attain maximum speed in his walking or running. Likewise it is fun for children to play around with big ideas. Young children just starting kindergarten are excited about becoming as smart as Mommy or Daddy now that they are in school. But would it make sense for a child to be immersed in a curriculum that was too big for him? How would he feel about getting to that wonderful place he expected "knowledge" to be? In the same way, a curriculum or program must fit the individual child if he is going to proceed at an appropriate, or comfortable, learning pace. This means that average, bright, brighter and brightest children cannot be expected to thrive on the same size ideas or activities. There cannot be one program that fits them all. There cannot be one curriculum (content), or method (process) or outcome (product) to fit them all.

As children grow older, you start buying them shoes for specific purposes, such as dress shoes, gym shoes, hiking boots, soccer cleats, ballerina slippers, etc. Likewise, as children grow older they have specific programming needs which fit their specific talents, like accelerated mathematics, music ensembles, varsity sports, research opportunities, etc. Whether based on the size or the nature of their talent, the same program will not fit all their needs.

One program cannot fit all, true. But in fairness, this is where the great difficulty lies in programming, and it is a complex dilemma.

4. Myth: Children do not know they are different unless someone tells them. And, if one child does something better than another, it will make the other child feel bad. In a kindergarten classroom, if one child knows how to tie shoes and another does not, should the one who knows the skill help the other? It is not uncommon to see children helping each other with skills like shoe-tying. The one who does not know how to tie shoes does not feel inferior if the children are left alone to share and grow naturally. And, the child who does know how to tie shoes feels neither superior nor in need of hiding this wonderful skill.

But what about differences in more school-related skills? If your 10 year old is ready for algebra or geometry, or more advanced math, should he be relearning multiplication and division with his chronological age peers, or joining older students who are learning a more advanced curriculum? When bright, brighter and brightest children are allowed to go at their own paces and are taught to respect children who proceed at slower paces, the slower ones do not feel inferior. In fact, usually (maybe openly, maybe secretly) they admire the brightest student, just as the football team admires its star fullback or the cross country team its fastest runner. They recognize and admire the star athlete's contribution without suffering a loss in their own self-esteem. If taught to value academics, they will also be proud of the brightest student's achievements without losing self-esteem. It is unhealthy to force children to believe that everyone is the same when individual differences are natural and inevitable.

Without anyone telling them, your bright preteens or teens know they are different. They know it when no one laughs at their jokes; they know it when no one wants to discuss serious topics such as ethnic wars or the consequences of nuclear proliferation; they know it when no one understands the excitement of their latest accomplishments; they know it socially and emotionally. School is not enough if they have not found kindred spirits. School is not enough if they are hiding their talents rather than letting them grow and bloom.

Responding to Talent Indicators — the Challenge

Schools are designed to provide a significant share of students' educational preparation for adult life. The challenge from a talent development perspective is for schools to provide the greatest educational fit possible for individuals who have many different learning characteristics, varied personality characteristics and different cultural, economic and social backgrounds. In order for schools to adequately educate the bright, brighter and brightest in particular, we suggest 10 propositions of excellence that should determine and undergird program development. Each proposition builds upon and varies (sometimes slightly) in meaning from the one that precedes it.

1. Healthy, *regular* programs in the schools define educational excellence and provide the foundation upon which programming for talented students should be built.

If schools develop a single program to meet the needs of the gifted, chances are that it might meet some of the needs of a very few bright students but not all the unique needs of many children with varying potential and specific talents. However, if a school is known to have a solid educational foundation based on standards such as enrichment opportunities for all students, high standardized test scores and great numbers of students successfully pursuing higher education goals, its teachers can build upon these successes to provide for the unique needs of their brightest students. The fact that you are reading this book may be an indication that you see some of the brightest are falling through the cracks. A key to real health in the school may be the willingness of educators to admit that their good foundation does not mean they are necessarily providing optimal programming for every child.

2. True excellence is attained only when the school adheres to the ideal of meeting differentiated, individual learning needs.

Most schools refer to this proposition in their mission statements. You have a right to ask your school principal, teachers and special services staff exactly how they are meeting the individual learning needs of your child. In parent-teacher conferences, ask for examples of where your child's curriculum is specifically geared to his strengths and his weaknesses. If you perceive your child's strengths differently than the teacher, be prepared to share samples of work your child has done at home or in the community that indicate talent in ways in which the teacher may be unaware. Give the teacher a chance to change curricular expectations based on the new information you have given. Find out what help exists for the teacher. If the needs of your child go beyond what can be expected in the regular classroom, you may need to talk with a gifted program specialist, the principal or even personnel on the district level. Responsibility for individual student needs extends beyond the individual teacher to everyone in the system who procedurally influences your child's school experience.

3. All students should have an equal opportunity for talent development each and every year in school.

Parents have no basis to dispute school personnel on the equity issue; equal opportunity for all children is not debatable in our democratic society. What is debatable, and will be very difficult to resolve, is the situation in which equal opportunity is confused with offering the same curriculum, the same activities, the same pace of learning to everyone. Heterogeneous grouping or inclusion of all students in one classroom according to all factors except age is currently popular. If your school advocates heterogeneous classes, especially for your talented preteens and teens, you must refer back to Proposition 2: asking for clarification of how differentiated individual needs are being met. Within what the school is presenting as its equitable framework, there must be a plan for how each child can advance according to individual learning needs. Equal opportunity for all means an equal opportunity for your child to advance one year in academic growth, whatever the school structure and whatever the student's presenting level of mastery.

4. Identification of gifted students should be redefined in the schools as talent assessment.

Talent assessment means that each child's learning characteristics and needs are constantly being considered in light of what he is doing in school. Every class, every club, every activity should match specific strengths, weaknesses and interests demonstrated in a particular discipline, field or curricular area. Unlike identification, which is usually viewed as a starting point only, talent assessment is a continuous process that determines a starting point, verifies ongoing appropriateness of the learning situation, evaluates outcomes and leads to continuous progress through the learning situation or into a new one. This can also be called *diagnostic-prescriptive assessment*, which means diagnostic testing followed by prescribed instruction (Stanley, 1984).

5. There should be a match between the learning characteristics of the student and the learning opportunities afforded through the curriculum.

Specialists in talent development do not contend that gifted students require a curriculum that differs in substance from that taught to other students. Rather, it is the pace and level of the curriculum that needs differentiation. The term *optimal match* describes the fit that should occur between any child's assessed abilities, demonstrated achievement, expressed interests and motivation and the pacing and level of instruction. When a child learns more rapidly or slowly than his age peers, a traditional one-size-fits-all lockstep curriculum in an age-grouped classroom will not match his learning needs. In fact, what we refer to as the traditional learning model — students divided by birth dates into classrooms confined within four walls — actually dates back to the industrial revolution. If you think about the days of the one-room rural classroom, you will find the origins of optimal match: "the permeability of the boundaries between various places of learning, flexibility and opportunities for early specialization" (Durden & Tangherlini, 1993, p. 6). We need to recapture the characteristics of institutional and instructional flexibility, in which children proceed at their own appropriate paces with a guide-on-the-side to point them to appropriate resources and to help them succeed.

6. Teachers should not have sole responsibility for the total talent development of their students.

In the early, and simpler, days of rural American education, the teacher did not have full responsibility for the development of the children in her charge. Parents, neighbors, church and community all played significant roles. Then, as people migrated to the cities, it was necessary to educate larger groups of students. To meet demands for education, the defined-by-age classroom was created. The teachers became the primary assessors of their students' learning needs and the primary guides to their learning fulfillment.

They shut their respective classroom doors at the beginning of the year and spewed out their products (the students) at the end.

Given today's complexity of society and schools, the kinds of out-of-school issues and problems students bring to school with them, the range of student strengths and weaknesses and the magnitude of the information explosion, it is now unreasonable to see teachers as the "be all" of every student's every learning moment. If the needs of the brightest students, along with the needs of all other students, are to be met totally in the regular classroom, something miraculous in terms of resources must occur. Teachers will require support systems that do not exist in most schools. Many different kinds of specialists will need to augment the efforts of regular classroom teachers. Teacher training will need to be more than a one-day shot in the arm by an outside expert. Good teachers can do a lot in the regular classroom; they can do more in that classroom if they have a strong support system and expertise in what it is they are expected to teach. But regular classroom teachers cannot do it all by themselves. Likewise, any school district cannot do it in isolation. As the old proverb suggests, it takes an entire village to educate a child.

7. Differentiated programming to meet varying talent-development needs cannot occur without adequate support functions in the school.

In the days of one-room schoolhouses, families and communities provided the resources necessary for the teacher to take students beyond the school walls. With today's complex school structure, there must be resources within the school itself that will allow a child to go beyond what can be learned within the confines of a single classroom. This support structure includes the following functions, which will be elaborated in Chapter 3:

- Coordination of specialized services or classes for children with different needs
- Ongoing staff development to teach teachers state-of-the-art ideas in content and techniques
- A talent assessment system that permeates learning in and beyond the regular classroom
- Parent involvement in assessment and nurturance of learning throughout the days and years
- A flexible-pacing policy that clarifies how children can proceed with continuous progress until they graduate from high school
- Counseling services for all children, not just those in physical or emotional crisis

The community still has an obligation to take a child even further. However, schools must often alert institutions and individuals of the community to the roles they can play. For example, it is not uncommon to hear business people say they would gladly be mentors, but no one ever asked them. Service clubs and local businesses often report that they would gladly fund a child to attend a special program, but they have not been asked. This points again to the need for coordination in helping teachers connect their students with a vast array of opportunities. Teachers do not have the time and should not bear the responsibility of doing this alone.

8. Talent development will require specialized opportunities beyond the classroom for many students.

Classroom teachers should recognize just how far they can take a talented student. If a teacher is offering an advanced curriculum designed specifically for students with advanced skills, knowledge, abilities and motivations, chances are this instructor can take them quite far. On the other hand, in a classroom in which a basic course is being taught to students of mixed abilities, skill-readiness and background interests, chances are the teacher can only take the fastest learners part of the way to where they need to go. Teachers should be aware of, willing and able to use resources beyond the classroom that will help the brighter and brightest students move beyond classroom limitations.

9. Flexible pacing, including acceleration, is the linchpin of comprehensive-integrated programming.

This proposition is full of buzz words and educational jargon that we believe the layperson needs to hear and understand. Most of the terms are self-explanatory when taken out of the educational context, and they are critical to our educational model for bright, brighter and brightest students when reinserted into the educational context.

Flexible pacing means any arrangement that allows each student to move forward in the curriculum as he masters content and skills. It allows variations in the instructional setting that lead to an optimal match for each student. For some students, flexible pacing means acceleration.

Acceleration means picking up speed. When we think of acceleration on the highway, we know that it is acceptable to accelerate within safe limits. On superhighways, multiple lanes are provided for varying rates of speed. The goal is to get into the best lane to match your speed needs. Likewise, in schools acceleration means picking up speed or increasing the pace of learning in one subject or more. If children of varying levels of ability and readiness are all forced to learn at the pace of the slowest, or even the average learner, they will not all reach levels of learning that match their speed needs. Students who could and should be traveling at faster paces will inevitably be slowed down. A professor who was offering advanced, fast-paced mathematics to mathematically talented middle-school students said, "This curriculum is not accelerated if you consider what these students should be learning. It is a perfect fit. It is only called accelerated because it is faster than what is offered in the schools." His students were in the passing lane, not the truck lane.

Comprehensive programming implies that there is something more complex than a one-size-fits-all program. It means that many different options are available through many different curricular paths to serve the talent-development needs of many different students. *Integrated programming* means that these options occur within the regular school day, as a part of the regular curriculum, and in relation to everything else that happens in school. Integrated programming considers the whole child within the whole learning structure. Taken together, *comprehensive-integrated programming* implies that options are sequential; options reach across, throughout and beyond school boundaries; options cross disciplines, age and grade levels, and kinds and degrees of talent; and options are carefully articulated and blended in a way that allows for continuous progress from kindergarten through high school.

If your school or district asserts that it has comprehensive-integrated programming, your child should not be working at slower than his ideal pace. Flexible pacing is the glue that holds the parts of the total programming model together. No matter how rigorous the curriculum and no matter how varied the opportunities for children to find the best fit, there should always be ways a child can accelerate within a specific talent area.

10. Excellence in education means rigorous content as well as challenging processes, competition as well as cooperation, differentiated outcomes as well as equality of opportunity, a varied pace and level of instruction, as well as high standards for all.

We tend to simplify education into an either/or decision-making framework. We should not consider it that way. We cannot pit course content against learning processes, because children need both. Yes, they need to learn how to think, but thinking does not occur in a vacuum. All too often in schools today, processes are taught in a vacuum. Process needs to be applied to content. And content needs to be rigorous enough to take students to a new level of knowledge.

We cannot pit cooperation against competition, because children need both. Competition can be healthy or unhealthy, depending on the way in which it is presented and handled. Students need healthy competition to spur their growth and development. They need to feel they are fairly and successfully competing within themselves as well as with others. We accept healthy competition in athletics and in adult society. We need to also accept healthy competition in school. Likewise, cooperative learning or teamwork can be healthy or unhealthy, depending on the way in which it is handled. Cooperation that has everyone doing the same task, in the same way, for the same purpose, makes no sense in the work world, and neither does it make sense in the classroom. Just as individual accomplishment, contribution and accountability are keys to success in the cooperative work environment, so must children have opportunity for individual accomplishment, contribution and accountability in a cooperative learning situation.

We cannot pit equality of opportunity against differentiation of outcomes. *Outcomes* is not a buzzword of the 90s. We have always had outcomes in school; we used to call them measurable learning objectives. Outcomes in adult work vary with the type and level of task undertaken. Yet high expectations and standards accompany these varied outcomes for individuals in the workplace. The results or outcomes of the business will be successful and profitable to the degree to which each worker is performing at an optimal level. In school, outcomes will be successful to the degree that students, too, can perform at their optimal levels.

We cannot pit having high standards for all against having a varied pace and level of instruction that will meet the demands of individual differences. Because we have lowered educational standards or expectations in general for students in this country, we now must reverse direction and raise the floor of our base standards and expectations. There is little argument that this is necessary. But for some students we have not only lowered the floor over the years, we have also lowered the ceiling. As the Talent Search model of assessment demonstrates, we can and must raise or even remove the ceiling of our curricular expectations. Children in this country are capable of going as fast as or faster than their counterparts in countries with much more rigorous learning expectations. We must expect more children to achieve at the top than we ever dreamed possible. Only when all of our students, including the brightest, are expected to work hard and master challenging knowledge and skills, will we attain academic excellence rather than "academic adequacy" (O'Connell Ross, 1993).

3-Promise for School Change

Responding to Talent Indicators — The Ideal

In the 1980s a pyramid model was introduced as a way of looking at promising practices for "educating able learners;" it was an outcome of what is called the Richardson Study of gifted education (Cox, Daniel & Boston,1985). Many schools, districts and state education departments have used some variation of this model to define how an educational system could meet the needs of bright, brighter and brightest students. The theoretical framework presented in Figures 1 and 2 is an adaptation of the pyramid developed for the Department of Public Instruction in Wisconsin (Clasen & Clasen, 1987; Schatz, 1989), presenting a visual model for implementation of the propositions presented in Chapter 2.

Figure 1 demonstrates the multifaceted nature and complexity of the model. At the base of the figure is the foundation of excellence — a healthy, regular program for all students. The four sides of the pyramid delineate all elements required for successful implementation:

1. Support roles
2. Support functions
3. Systematic and continuous programming options
4. Evaluation

Figure 2 presents us with a more complete overview of programming options and, by continuing to show the support-function side of the pyramid, demonstrates that these options must be integrated with the total school program. This means that programming options cannot stand alone. As with the pyramids of Egypt, all four of the model's triangles, standing solidly together, are necessary to provide the strength of the total geometric structure. The whole becomes greater than the sum of the parts.

We know many excellent teachers who became very excited when introduced to the pyramid model, feeling that it aptly defined education as they saw it and delineated classroom instruction as they practiced it. But with regular classroom differentiation at the bottom of the programming-options side of the pyramid, sometimes teachers' initial reaction to the schematic is one of fear or cynicism. Since this is the component that involves them

Figure 1

WISCONSIN'S COMPREHENSIVE INTEGRATED GIFTED PROGRAMMING MO

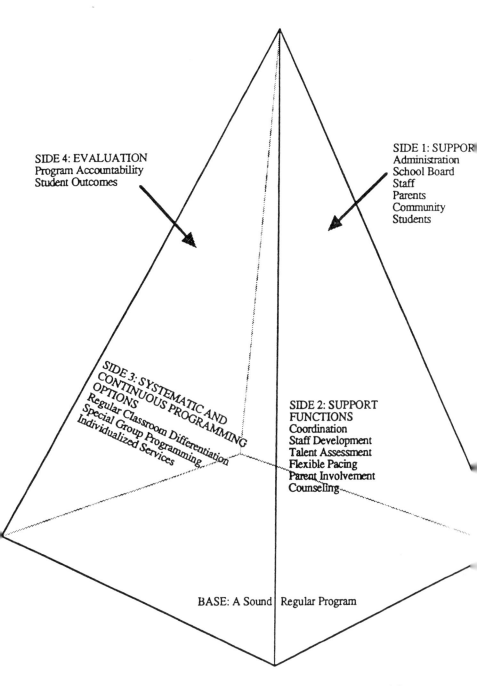

SIDE 4: EVALUATION
Program Accountability
Student Outcomes

SIDE 1: SUPPOR
Administration
School Board
Staff
Parents
Community
Students

SIDE 3: SYSTEMATIC AND
CONTINUOUS PROGRAMMING
OPTIONS
Regular Classroom Differentiation
Special Group Programming
Individualized Services

SIDE 2: SUPPORT
FUNCTIONS
Coordination
Staff Development
Talent Assessment
Flexible Pacing
Parent Involvement
Counseling

BASE: A Sound Regular Program

PREMISE: All students will develop to their fullest potential

Figure 2

WISIN'S COMPREHENSIVE INTEGRATED GIFTED PROGRAMMING MODEL

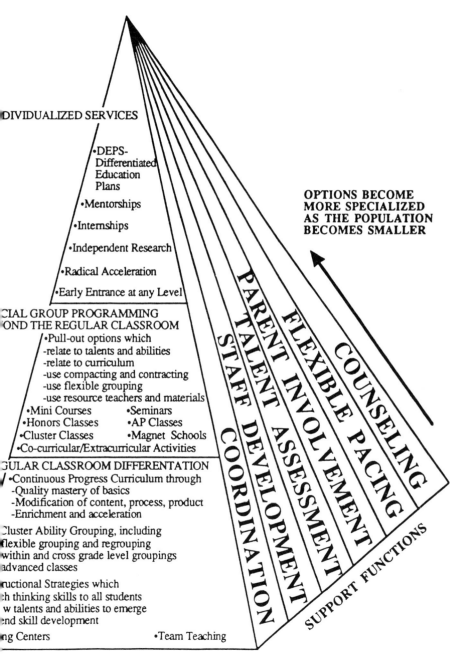

OPTIONS BECOME
MORE SPECIALIZED
AS THE POPULATION
BECOMES SMALLER

INDIVIDUALIZED SERVICES

- •DEPS- Differentiated Education Plans
- •Mentorships
- •Internships
- •Independent Research
- •Radical Acceleration
- •Early Entrance at any Level

SPECIAL GROUP PROGRAMMING
BEYOND THE REGULAR CLASSROOM

- •Pull-out options which
  - -relate to talents and abilities
  - -relate to curriculum
  - -use compacting and contracting
  - -use flexible grouping
  - -use resource teachers and materials
- •Mini Courses   •Seminars
- •Honors Classes   •AP Classes
- •Cluster Classes   •Magnet Schools
- •Co-curricular/Extracurricular Activities

REGULAR CLASSROOM DIFFERENTIATION

- •Continuous Progress Curriculum through
  - -Quality mastery of basics
  - -Modification of content, process, product
  - -Enrichment and acceleration

- Cluster Ability Grouping, including
  flexible grouping and regrouping
  within and cross grade level groupings
  advanced classes

- Instructional Strategies which
  -teach thinking skills to all students
  -allow talents and abilities to emerge
  -extend skill development

- Learning Centers   •Team Teaching

COORDINATION
STAFF DEVELOPMENT
TALENT ASSESSMENT
PARENT INVOLVEMENT
FLEXIBLE PACING
COUNSELING

SUPPORT FUNCTIONS

PROGRAMMING OPTIONS

Teens With Talent 25

most directly, the implication they draw is that the full responsibility for talent development will be theirs. Cynicism is justified when a district or school is suffering from the "We're not doing that part" syndrome. This means that teachers and, moreover, administrators in such a district are separating the parts from the whole, adopting some of the components of the pyramid and ignoring others. The model will not work if programming is understood as some enrichment for all rather than differentiation for many in the regular classroom. The model will not work if a district puts all its emphasis on the regular classroom aspect of the pyramid to the exclusion of the more selective and individualized opportunities. Nor will the model work if the emphasis is placed on the whole programming-options side to the exclusion of the others. Unless there are adequate support functions to assure success for teachers working with a wide variety of students in the classroom, and unless there are more specialized options that will ensure that the brightest students can "move ahead as they master content and skills" (Cox, et al., 1985, p. 158), the model will not work; it will remain only an ideal.

Understanding Enrichment versus Acceleration

The pyramid provides a framework for discussing and choosing promising practices and understanding what an ideal talent-development school might be like. Defining the concepts of enrichment and acceleration provides a framework for understanding specific methods or strategies for instruction within the pyramid model.

To *enrich* means to improve or to enhance. Whether we are motivated by the poor American showings on international test data, complaints of business leaders regarding our untrained national work force or the grim realities of turned-off, dropped-out young people in our schools and on our streets, this fact remains: we, as a nation, need to enrich curriculum. This enrichment should take into consideration necessary educational improvements for all students as well as those needed for the highly able.

There are two kinds of *enrichment*. The first is enhancement of content for *all* students. This should be reflected at the base of the pyramid as a part of the sound, regular program as well as in the regular classroom. For instance, teaching of thinking skills and the use of learning centers are examples of instructional strategies that should be used to enhance learning for all students. The second is enhancement of content for *some* students. This enrichment is more specialized, matching learning options to differentiated-learner interests and needs, and most often occurs at the "regular-classroom differentiation" level. It includes the use of cluster grouping or the modification of content, process and product. Enrichment for *some* students should also occur beyond the regular classroom as one continues up the pyramid.

One legitimate criticism of gifted pull-out programs has been that they offer enrichment for some students when that enrichment should have been for all. With this model of comprehensive-integrated programming, it is important to establish that any enrichment occurring in small groups or for individuals is designed specifically to meet the needs and interests of those students. Such enrichment would not work for all because the students for whom it was not intended would find it too challenging or complex, or not matched to their specific talents or strengths. This would endanger rather than enhance their learning environment.

As noted in Chapter 2, to *accelerate* means to hasten or to go faster. It seems paradoxical that we are viewed internationally as a fast-paced nation of people living fast-paced lives, yet through the decades we have slowed the pace of our instruction. Until all our students are learning at a pace that is fast enough to meet both their needs and those of our nation, acceleration will remain a necessary component of schooling.

Acceleration Across the Pyramid

John Feldhusen (1990) writes, "There has been too much emphasis on the base (of the pyramid) and some enrichment for all." He continues by discussing the need for more emphasis on acceleration and special classes for the brightest students if the pyramid model is to work. Although the pyramid depicted in Figure 2 unquestionably encompassed enrichment, it was intended to embrace acceleration as well. Figure 3 is a clearer visual representation of how acceleration could be incorporated across the pyramid.

Looking at the right side of this representation, we return to the proposition articulating *flexible pacing* as the linchpin. The original dictum of the Richardson Study still holds: students must move forward in the curriculum as they demonstrate mastery of content and skills (Cox, et al., 1985). For many high potential youngsters, this dictum means going at a faster pace, starting with what we will call *accelerated enrichment*. Stanley (1976) clarified what is meant by this when he stated that the more relevant and excellent the enrichment program, the more it calls for acceleration for some students. By placing accelerated enrichment in the regular classroom differentiation section as we have done here, we are suggesting, as did Cox & Daniel (1988), that rather than

Figure 3

ACCELERATION ACROSS THE PYRAMID

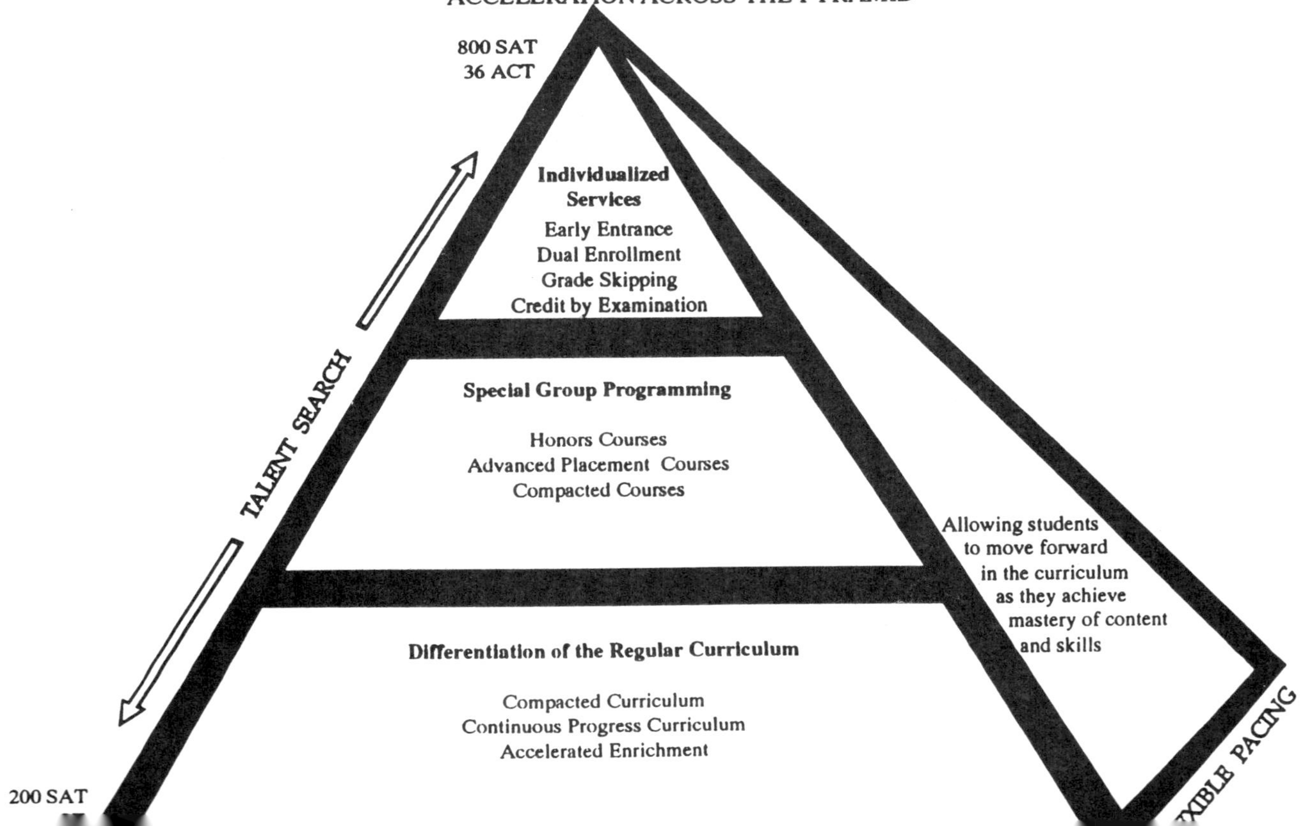

800 SAT
36 ACT

Individualized Services

Early Entrance
Dual Enrollment
Grade Skipping
Credit by Examination

Special Group Programming

Honors Courses
Advanced Placement Courses
Compacted Courses

Differentiation of the Regular Curriculum

Compacted Curriculum
Continuous Progress Curriculum
Accelerated Enrichment

Allowing students
to move forward
in the curriculum
as they achieve
mastery of content
and skills

FLEXIBLE PACING

TALENT SEARCH

200 SAT

moving bright students up to advanced content, the advanced content can sometimes be moved down to the bright students. But, as stated earlier, this does not mean that all acceleration can take place in the regular classroom; rather, some can when teachers have the needed support system.

On the left side of Figure 3, we see the use of Talent Search for assessment purposes. The use of Talent Search here is not meant to limit acceleration across the pyramid to the middle grades, nor to students who can demonstrate their potential through standardized tests. As mentioned earlier, the concept of an out-of-level assessment can be applied across all grade levels and across all talent areas. In most states the Talent Search program has now been extended to students in 5th and 6th grades, and in at least one state, Iowa, to students in grade 4. A reading specialist might administer a 5th-grade achievement test to a 1st grader who reads fluently. An art teacher might evaluate a student's portfolio. Once a student's out-of-level profile is established, the information gleaned from the process should be used for planning appropriate instructional levels, methods and materials throughout the rest of the precollegiate years.

Students who are in the top 5% of achievement on grade-level standardized tests will most likely require accelerated enrichment in the regular classroom. Middle school students who are scoring at or above the mean for college-bound seniors through programs such as Talent Search will most likely require advanced courses or specialized interest groups taught at an accelerated pace beyond that of the regular classroom. Documentation from a diagnostic-prescriptive assessment will often provide evidence for the necessity of such courses. Furthermore, performance at the very top of an out-of-level assessment procedure provides evidence that individualized services beyond even the special groupings are also required. From an acceleration perspective, it can be expected that middle school students will be involved with options at the high school level. Whether their talent is in mathematics, as demonstrated by greater than 500 on the math SAT at age 10 to 13; or in dance, as demonstrated by a professionally-rated audition as a young teen; or in a completely different talent field as demonstrated by a reliable out-of-level tool within that field, these top performers may even need to graduate early. Their passions and their need to progress rapidly, whether mentally or physically, will dictate the need for acceleration across the pyramid.

Differentiated Education Plans (DEPs)

Federal law guarantees children with disabilities the right to a free appropriate public education as specified in an Individualized Education Program (IEP). If, as we suggested earlier, all schools state in their missions that they will meet the individual needs of all children, it follows that an IEP should be the right of any individual child. This puts the focus of the educational process where it should be: on the individual student.

Because IEPs are not federally regulated for our brightest students, we will share a euphemism that focuses more on the child and the process and less (by association) on paperwork and regulations. This is the concept of *Differentiated Education Plans (DEPs)*.

A DEP, then, is an IEP in a simpler form, a plan that expands upon the diagnostic-prescriptive assessment model. It consists of an assessment of a student's abilities and needs, a prescribed program of educational objectives and services based on that assessment and a procedure for monitoring and evaluating the success of the program. It also provides for updating, as the student moves through the educational system. A DEP utilizes a team approach and should be signed by an official from the school, the parent(s) and the student. The following two case studies were described by gifted program coordinator, Mary Kay Miller (1991), and demonstrate how the process can work.

The first case involves a 7th-grade boy. This student and his family had been considering grade skipping into grade 9 for the upcoming school year. Toward the end of the boy's 7th-grade year, the school district's gifted-education department was contacted by the student's family. As a result of the family's initial communication, the coordinator of the program set up a team meeting for the last week of school, including gifted-education department personnel, middle and high school principals and counselors, classroom teachers, the student and his parents. It was also determined that a written DEP should be developed for the student. DEPs in this district consist of three major sections: 1) What We Know, 2) What We Plan (or Options) and 3) Considerations.

The "What We Know" section presented a history of the student's academic success in school, including: academic grade reports, Cognitive Abilities Test results, Otis-Lennon Test results, achievement test scores, American College Test (ACT) scores, a comparison of the percent of Midwest Talent Search students scoring at or below the student's scores and charts interpreting the student's ACT scores and learning needs. The "What We Plan" section consisted of four options: placement in 9th grade, subject acceleration, independent study opportunities through the middle school and maintaining the status quo. "Considerations" included background facts on grade skipping and acceleration, such as when and under what circumstances the desired accelerative option was appropriate.

At the close of the team meeting, all attending personnel signed the Differentiated Education Plan (DEP) agreeing to the student's choice of being placed in high school the next year. At the meeting, the parents and the high school counselor began to discuss and plan appropriately accelerated high school course work. The day after the meeting, the secondary gifted and talented resource teacher took the student to the high school to familiarize him with the school.

The second case concerns a 7th-grade girl. She had extremely high verbal scores through Talent Search, indicating that new programming options in English should be considered. Several meetings were held in which the student, her family, the school administrator, middle and high school counselors, an 8th grade English teacher, the school psychologist and coordinator for gifted education were involved. The student's family requested that an additional option be included with the district's options on the "What We Plan" section of the DEP. Ultimately the student and her family chose a combination of two options: subject acceleration to high school English while taking the rest of her classes in middle school (*dual enrollment*) and their own option, which included completion of a five-year academic plan based on the student's personalized worksheets from her involvement in Talent Search. Further steps included meetings with the high school counselor and English teacher as well as arranging transportation that would best facilitate the dual-enrollment arrangement.

These cases show how a district can build a model based on flexible pacing. The results were significant not only for the individual students, but for the entire system which, through each case, developed procedures to be used for other students. A school district must back up its philosophical beliefs in the comprehensive-integrated programming model not only with adequate resources and personnel, but also with adequate policies. For instance, as soon as the aforementioned district started accelerating students based on their DEPs, credit for advanced classes taken early or through a university and requests for early graduation became issues. Because school board-approved policy had never been developed for either issue, such policy had to be advanced, studied and ultimately approved.

The question now becomes: Is school enough if a district, like this one, implements the comprehensive-integrated programming model described in this chapter? The answer is no, even if the model works to the best possible advantage of every talented student. By definition, the model clearly dictates that meeting the needs of the brightest students requires going beyond the four walls of a classroom and beyond the walls of the school building. Next we will examine ways for teens with talent, whatever their intellectual level, to take advantage of extra-programming options, to connect those options back to the schools in order to maximize their total learning experience and to build upon their previous experiences as they move from precollegiate to post-secondary education.

4-Going Beyond: Extra-Programming Options

This chapter explores extra-programming options which promote and encourage learning as well as foster appropriate intellectual growth, social development and formation of character. These options can be initiated by schools, parents or both and may be used as enrichment or acceleration. Both formal and informal opportunities are cited, and we encourage you and your teen to use these ideas as a beginning point in your discovery of additional alternatives.

Many of these options can be considered for high school credit in some districts. High school credit can even be granted to middle school students if content is at an appropriately high level. This differs greatly among districts and states, depending on policies and laws.

A family's provision for the needs of an academically talented child does cost more, both in time and money. Students at either end of the spectrum from average require different resources. These take energy and time to discover as well as money to obtain or utilize. However, there are ways to keep costs low and have the whole family benefit.

Before we discuss these extra-programming options, let us examine two misconceptions about decision-making that affect learning beyond school.

1. Misconception: *Parent says, "My child works hard in school all day during the school year, therefore he should have the opportunity to just have fun the rest of the time."* Formal schooling is required for only 12 to 16 years of our lives, yet learning occurs throughout a lifetime. How open we are to learning will have an impact upon any job we hold, and our attitudes toward learning will ultimately affect opportunities and career choices. And, bright students often perceive more learning as fun. Sylvia Rimm (1990) refers to the joy of "intrinsic learning" and states that parents are the best models for lifelong attitudes about learning (p. 269). If parents send the message that education only takes place in school, then it should be no surprise if their children deny any intellectual passions and suppress any further interest in academic pursuits.

2. Misconception: *You can never get too much of a good thing.* Often, we hear about the pushy parent whose child is programmed for every waking moment. However, sometimes our bright, brighter and brightest children are interested in so many things that they over-program themselves. Parents need to monitor their children's degree of involvement and use good judgment in determining how many classes, sports, clubs, as well as hours of employment, are reasonable at any particular age. Helping your child make choices, perhaps by first talking about criteria, is also a form of learning. Remember that some down-time, sometimes called boredom by our children, can serve as valuable periods for creativity, relaxation, assimilation of thoughts and rejuvenation.

Tasks and Chores Around the Home

One obvious place for extra-programming options to begin is right in your home. Home learning may often be spontaneous, based on opportunities that present themselves. Such an opportunity is illustrated by Rick, a high school senior. His parents hired him one summer to build a prefabricated utility shed on their property, paying him the difference between that one and a fully assembled unit that could be delivered. Rick had never built anything with wood before, so he needed to read and follow directions and interpret them for the intended location. Having recently completed college calculus, Rick now had to apply math to a real product. He also had to learn to use the tools of the trade to measure, cut and install a window, door, floor and roof. His summer discoveries included different ways to think when calculating on paper versus calculating in the field, with consideration for such things as the width of the saw blade and drill bit. When completed, Rick had a well-deserved sense of pride in his product. He learned many practical applications which made his formal education more purposeful, and his self-esteem increased through his own real effort.

Certainly bright children should not have more or fewer of the shared household duties than any other child, nor necessarily be exempt from any tasks. However, there are many home situations in which they can be challenged with real-life problems. Can we make a balanced nutritional dinner for our family of four for $8? How much lumber should we buy to build a fence to go around the backyard? Where can we cut corners in our budget to pay for that new VCR we all want, and how long will it take to save enough money for it? How do you create a household budget using a computer spread sheet?

Family Conversation

Look for opportunities for family sharing to keep the lines of communication open, thus boosting self-esteem in all siblings and establishing value in each of their contributions. Bright students need to be acknowledged, need to understand how to appreciate people with less academic horsepower, and need to know they are important contributing members of their family community. These young people also have an uncanny level of sensitivity to nonverbal communication. This sensitivity can add to their feelings of insecurity by causing them to view themselves as different, weird or even stupid. Talking and sharing within the family will help them understand what others are really thinking and thus will help them understand themselves.

Bright children need to practice good communication skills which include speaking, listening and practicing patience. It is sometimes hard for adults to remember that just because a child is very bright, it does not mean he is automatically good at areas of skill development; sharing and communication techniques are acquired skills. Sharing, however, does need some orchestration. Two or three meals a week may be mandatory for all to attend. Or perhaps an evening is set aside with no television or video games. During these times, conversation on areas of interest to each member of the family can be initiated by the parents. Mom talks about some of the problems and satisfactions that have occurred at work or home. Dad relates an experience from the conference he attended or his day at home. Children may be asked what is happening with their friends, school or outside activities. Politics, world and community happenings, and planning for family events are other important topics for discussion. This time could also be used to determine distribution of household tasks. Parents can use the opportunity to demonstrate that they have both abilities and limitations. A well-placed "I don't know" might encourage children to find some answers and educate Dad or Mom. Family conversation fosters true development of understanding of others, tolerance, ways to contribute to the family community and appreciation of feelings and thoughts.

Travel

Opportunities for exploration can be simple as well as elaborate and need not cost much money. Day trips offer great options. If you live in a rural area, a trip to a city may be exciting, and vice versa. Look for connections to interests and strengths as well as potential career ideas. A picnic at a riverside park can present the opportunity for studying rocks, observing plants and animals, for connecting mathematics to the power of water flow or electric potential, or for determining the chemistry of the water. Sketching scenery or writing about the area are also possibilities. Visiting an amusement park could start some discussion of physics. Children of varying ages can assist in planning both long and short trips. They can help decide what to see, chart routes, check budgets and make reservations. Someone can do research on the area history, too. A travel opportunity for older children might offer opportunities for independent study. Arranging a contract beforehand with a teacher could result in a student earning high school credit through research, writing and/or product development connected to part of the travel.

There are also many opportunities for youth to travel to different countries. Trips can range from a few weeks during the summer to a full year in length. An option for the student who finishes all high school course work in less than four years but does not yet want to start college could involve a foreign travel program. Some require a knowledge of the country's language, whereas others do not; students may go independently or with a group, and many programs offer the chance to stay with families in the new country. Again, high school credit for this type of experience may be a possibility. Your school system or a community organization such as Rotary may already have established foreign exchange programs. The United States government publishes an annotated list of programs offering travel abroad.

• *Advisory List of International Educational Travel and Exchange Programs,* Council on Standards for International Educational Travel, 1906 Association Dr., Reston VA 22091; 703/860-5317.

Contests and Competitions

Your child can test his abilities by entering contests and competitions in his areas of strength and interest. Teachers often have information on contests that are local, state-wide or national in scope. Contests and competitions for groups or for individuals are also listed in youth and specialty magazines. This type of activity forces a student to polish his skills and gain awareness of all necessary components of competition; for example, neatness, completeness, creativity, method of presentation. Some to consider are:

• *Academic Decathlon* — High school juniors and seniors compete in teams of students with grade point averages of A, B and C. Different themes are introduced each year covering 10 content areas. PO Box 5169, Cerritos CA 90703-5169; 310/809-4995, FAX 310/809-4111.

• *American Express Geography Competition* — Critical thinking, geography and writing skills are used by students, grades 6-12, to solve an authentic task. The results are submitted for competition for award monies totaling $100,000. PO Box 672227, Marietta GA 30067-9077; 800/395-GLOBE, ask for *Atlas Map*.

• *The Citizen Bee* — American political and cultural history, government, geography, economics and current events are part of this competition for high school students. Educational Outreach, Close Up Foundation, 44 Canal Center Plaza, Alexandria VA 22314; 703/706-3300.

• *Daughters of the American Revolution History Essay Contest* — Each year public and parochial school principals receive information on this contest for students in grades 5-8. Essays based on the yearly history theme must be submitted by January 1. Contact your school principal.

• *Future Problem Solving* — This year-long program is a competition for students in grades 4-12. Students working in teams submit written solutions to complex scientific and social problems of the future. Judging occurs at the state, national and international levels. The methods of problem solving can be taught to entire classrooms. 318 W. Ann St., Ann Arbor MI 48104; 313/998-7377.

• *JETS, Inc. (Junior Engineering Technical Society)* — Precollege engineering career guidance, competitions and the *JETS Report* newsletter are all sponsored by this organization. 1420 King Street, Suite 405, Alexandria VA 22314-2794; 703/548-5387, FAX 703/548-0769, e-mail jets@nas.edu
WorldWideWeb http: \\www.asee.org\external\jets

• *Mathcounts Foundation* — Here is the opportunity for good math students in grades 7-8 to be challenged. Principals and math department teachers receive materials each year on this regional, state and national competition held in the spring. Mathcounts materials may also be used in the regular classroom. 1420 King St., Alexandria VA 22314; 703/684-2828, e-mail mcounts@nspe.org

• *Mock Trial Tournament* — Teams of students in grades 9-12 can test their critical thinking and public speaking skills in the atmosphere of a real-life trial situation. Contact your State Bar of Lawyers.

• *National Olympiads include Continental Mathematics League, Current Events League (National Social Studies Olympiad), National Geography Olympiad, National Language Arts Olympiad, National Science Olympiad and the National Social Studies Olympiad* —Teams at all grade levels compete at their home school site in the desired curriculum area.

Problem solving and analytical reasoning are integral to each discipline. PO Box 5477, Hauppauge NY 11788-0121; 516/265-4792.

• *National Written & Illustrated by... Awards Contest for Students* — This is an opportunity for students, ages 6-19, to compete for publication of a book which they have both written and illustrated. Send a self-addressed stamped envelope for instructions and an application form. Landmark Editions, Inc., PO Box 4469, 1402 Kansas Ave., Kansas City MO 64127; 816/241-4919.

• *Odyssey of the Mind* — Teams of five students and two alternates in grade categories are formed to compete in both long-term and spontaneous problem solving. Regional, state and national competitions are held each spring. Students are judged on creativity, originality, presentation style and the success of their long-term problem solution, along with the number of spontaneous answers to a short-term problem. This is a hands-on active competition. There are also OM Enrichment Programs available during the summer. OM Association, PO Box 547, Glassboro NJ 08028; 609/881-1603, FAX 609/881-3596.

• *Optimist International Oratorical Contest* — This contest is run annually by local Optimist Clubs for children under age 16. Contact a local Optimist Club member for more information.

• *Westinghouse Science Talent Search* — This scholarship competition is for students in their last year of high school. A written report on a student's independent research project is the basis for national recognition, which includes a large monetary award. Many students have worked on their projects for one or more years. 1719 N Street, NW, Washington DC 20036; 202/785-2255.

• *Young Astronaut Council* — Essay, art, math and science competitions, both locally and nationally, can be entered by local chapters. Available for preschool through junior high school students, it is designed to promote the study of science, mathematics and related subjects. 1308 19th St., NW, Washington DC 20036; 202/682-1984.

Seminars
Many libraries, universities, colleges and museums offer seminars in special-interest areas on weekends, weekday evenings or during the summer. These enrichment opportunities are great ways to expose your child to a new field or reinforce a subject that already interests him. They are also a good means of career exploration. As a word of caution, it is usually a mistake to have a child take a class in something he dislikes or in which he is not

particularly apt. These are meant to be enjoyable classes with no pressure, experiences in which participants share their love of continued learning with others. However, if your child has low self-motivation but you know he likes the subject matter, it might be appropriate to try to encourage participation. He will meet others with similar interests, may find new friends and may be sparked to learn more on his own. It might be particularly hard for a middle school student to attend a special program alone due to adolescent ideas of what is socially acceptable. Parent counseling will need to be done with care.

There may be occasions when you want your child to be in a special class offered for adults. Perhaps there is an advanced astronomy seminar being offered and your son has already built his own telescope. You may try calling the instructor and explaining the situation or, better yet, have your son make the call. Perhaps both you and your child could attend together if the instructor voices safety concerns.

Enrichment Classes

The number of enrichment classes offered for bright students outside the regular school day continues to grow across the nation. Enrichment classes are offered to enhance a student's learning in fun ways. These would be similar to the seminars discussed above, but longer. Classes may be run more like a summer camp, with the focus on academics, or offered a few hours per week over a four- to eight-week period. There may be a residential component during the summer, or students may commute on a daily basis. In these programs, learning usually occurs through many hands-on activities and experiences. Subjects range from arts and literature to music, math, science, computers and culture. The emphasis is on active learning in a relaxed setting.

Newspapers often list class opportunities in your area. (There are also some references listed in Appendix A to help you start your search.)

Accelerated Classes

These classes challenge a bright student to work at a pace that is more consistent with his quick learning ability. Students often need to meet high academic criteria before being accepted into such programs. Curriculum is covered at a much faster pace than in most schools and, in most cases, there is better retention of the material covered by these academically talented students. They remain actively involved rather than becoming bored and tuning out. As an example of the quickened pace, a three-week summer class in Japanese allows a student to complete the material taught in a one-year high school course. This sounds unbelievable; but for our brighter students it is not only attainable, but challenging and fun. (See Chapter 5 for more information on Summer Residency Programs.)

The most common form of accelerated classes occurs in mathematics. At the University of Wisconsin-Eau Claire, two-hour Saturday classes are held during the school year for qualified students in grades 7-9. In two years, students complete four years of high school mathematics (Rolland & Schuster, 1988). In three-week summer programs held around the country (e.g., Wisconsin Center for Academically Talented Youth, Northwestern University, Johns Hopkins University), a structured individually-paced math class allows a student to complete a minimum of one year of high school course work. Stanford University, through the Education Program for Gifted Youth (EPGY), offers self-paced and individualized math, science and writing classes using computers, CD-ROM, e-mail and telephones. (See Appendix A for contacts on these programs.)

Other accelerated classes may be equivalent to college courses, such as computer programming, geopolitics, logic and anthropology. Some of the above-mentioned programs also offer full-credit college programming for precollege students, either through summer classes, correspondence courses or electronic media.

Some students receive high school credit for these accelerated programs, whereas others do not. Because individual school districts decide issues of credit, policies vary greatly across the country. At a minimum, students should not have to repeat courses with similar curriculum content in their home schools. Also, this experience should be appropriately documented in official cumulative school folders and included on any college application forms.

What if your child has a bad experience with a class or does not like it? Find out what really happened. Was the class poorly run? Was the curriculum too easy? Or, if this was the first time your child was challenged, was he feeling inadequate and scared of failure when faced with difficult material? Often problems have nothing to do with learning, and he should be encouraged to try another accelerated class. One mother stated that her daughter hated a veterinary class taken through a summer program, and the mother was most grateful. The girl had wanted to be a veterinarian, but through the class she saw what the job really entailed and did not find it as glamorous as she envisioned. Mom said it was the best money she ever spent in helping her daughter eliminate a career choice. After the same course, another parent was pleased that his daughter decided that she definitely wanted to be a veterinarian. This girl proceeded to find a volunteer job working in a veterinary clinic.

Other Community-based Programs
Many bright students thrive on some of the more common enrichment experiences offered in a community and geared to certain age groups, such as 4-H, scouting, church and Junior Achievement. There are those bright students, however, who may have an interest or hobby and are unable to find "soul mates." Parents may want to help their teen form a club or group with individuals who have similar interests. In this case, age may not be the deciding factor for membership. Examples of possible clubs are: chess, railroad, computers and astronomy. *The Encyclopedia of Associations*, 30th Edition (Fischer C. A., & Schwartz, C. A., Detroit: Gale Research), lists a vast array of organizations, giving short descriptions about the organization as well as contacts. A sampling of some organizations listed in this resource book are:
• *Young Entomologists Society, Inc.*, 1915 Peggy Place, Lansing MI 48910-2553; 517/887-0499.
• *Teen Association of Model Railroaders (TAMR)*, 1800 E. 38th St., Oakland CA 94602-1720; 510/482-8760.
• *International Society of Worldwide Stamp Collectors*, Rt. 1, Box 69A, Caddo Mills TX 75135; 903/527-3957.

Most organizations and the highly motivated people operating them offer wonderful opportunities. Parents and children need to be creative, flexible and open to these new adventures. However, even with children in their teens, we must insert a word of caution. Please be aware of the health and safety issues when encouraging your child to join with people, both other children and adults, who are unknown to you. Seek trustworthy references in all these situations.
Many of the opportunities mentioned in this chapter are available to students without much school coordination. There are usually fees, but be sure to inquire about scholarships. Many organizations offer financial help for minority and low income students. Parents have also found creative ways to help their children attend costly special programs by matching dollar for dollar what a student can earn, encouraging relatives to contribute with birthday and holiday money gifts or finding local community organizations to sponsor their child (Lions Clubs, Rotary, Kiwanis, professional groups, the parent's workplace or a local business or industry). Some school districts also have funds to help students with special learning needs; gifted and talented

students should qualify and be eligible for such funds. Sometimes a student who has received financial assistance will be asked to share his experience with his sponsor through an oral or written report.

Post-secondary Options

If you are fortunate enough to have an institution of higher learning nearby, there are many advantages for high school students in taking college courses. Courses can be taken during the summer, in the evening, on Saturday morning or even during the school day with the cooperation of the high school. Any college credit students earn is "banked" until they enter college full time. It is also possible that students can earn dual credit from high school and college simultaneously. They are considered "special students" at the college or university and may need to meet special entrance criteria. Usually, high school juniors and seniors have the maturity and background to be successful in this situation, but there are also circumstances in which first and second year high school students, or even those at the middle school level, can appropriately take college courses. Because of the proliferation of accelerated math programs, it is not uncommon for high school freshmen to have completed all their high school math and be ready for college calculus. Some then attend courses at a local college for three semesters of calculus and go on to higher mathematics with great success. Others take these courses through correspondence programs, distance learning or in their high school, if scheduling permits. Students must understand, however, that grades earned in college will be permanent college grades. If they get high school credit as well, the grade may also be included in their high school Grade Point Average (GPA).

Taking college courses early gives students a jump on college. They learn a little about how colleges work and what kinds of study skills are needed. Having credits banked may allow new college students to enroll in classes earlier than peers, thus getting into required classes that are often filled. It may even have an impact on students' ability to graduate from college in four years or less, when a five-year bachelor's degree is becoming more common. Most important may be the idea that your high school student is staying involved in learning when high school may no longer be challenging.

High schools are also offering college classes in-house. These may be College Board "Advanced Placement" classes, in which students take a rigorous nationally-guided curriculum and then have the opportunity to take a standardized test in the spring. Or, there may be joint efforts with local colleges to offer college courses such as freshman English to high school seniors in place of the fourth year high school English class.

Alternative Means of Study

There are other flexible ways for talented students to go beyond the normal high school curriculum. We recommend that any alternative means of study be with high school cooperation, if possible, and that concerns regarding credit and placement be discussed in the beginning. Here are a few more alternatives:

• *Mentorship* — the deliberate linking of a student who has the need and ability to pursue a topic of personal interest in depth, breadth or at a fast pace with a knowledgeable adult who can serve as a role model in a one-to-one learning relationship. The subject area to be covered, length of time to be spent with the mentor, and expectations and guidelines for mentor and student are usually prearranged and may be written into a formal contract signed by all parties.

• *Independent study* — an opportunity for a student to work by himself at his own pace in a set curriculum. The curriculum may be equivalent to a unit, a semester or a year of work. A student who embarks on independent study must have a professional or an educator as facilitator, a person who will meet with him on a prearranged schedule for support, guidance and assistance.

• *Distance Learning* — education via television. One teacher can offer a subject to a few students in many different schools. Usually two-way audio is available for interactive discussions. In some instances, two-way video is also available. Broadcast distances vary from national to small-area distribution. School districts usually arrange for or subscribe to this type of service. This is a good way for rural students to have access to opportunities generally found in more populated regions.

• *Correspondence Courses* — curriculum offered by teachers to students over a large geographic area. Historically, the mail system has been the means of communication between student and teacher. Students set their own pace of learning, though there may be a maximum time requirement for completing work. This mode of learning is often offered through college and university extensions with college credit available.

• *Classes via Computer* — opportunities for students to work in a set curriculum but at their own speed, using computers or computer terminals as their instructional bases. One or more students may be working on the same curriculum, on different computers, but may be at different steps in the learning process. Curriculum may be on a computer software package, the student may be linked to another educational facility via modem (e-mail or Internet) or some combination, for example, Stanford University's Education Program for Gifted Youth (EPGY). This may also be described as distance learning, independent study or correspondence classes.

Other Resources

There are many other resources to explore for more options. Schools and teachers constantly receive information on opportunities. If you express your interest to the school, people there would probably be very happy to pass materials on to you. In fact, schools might welcome parent volunteers who are willing to organize and run a clearinghouse of extra-programming options. Libraries also have catalogs listing programs for all ages. Two other resources you may want to investigate are:

• *Directory of American Youth Organizations.* (1996). Free Spirit Publishing, Inc., 400 First Avenue North, Suite 616, Minneapolis MN 55401-1730; 800/735-7323.

• *Educational Opportunity Guide.* Talent Identification Program, Duke University, PO Box 40077, Durham NC 27706-0077.

A wise person once said that luck is opportunity meeting preparation. Taking advantage of opportunities now begins your child's preparation to meet the opportunities of the future.

5-Summer Residency Programs

Although many parents will readily accept that school is not enough and extra-programming options are both important and accessible, they often hesitate when it comes to consideration of summer programming options, particularly academic summer programs or camps. The comments of one parent explain why you, educators and even your teens themselves should read this chapter:

*(My daughter) attended her first summer residential program because of her love of the subject matter covered by the course. She — and we — did **not** expect the overwhelming experience of a strong, substantive academic challenge in the context of a supportive network: committed, highly skilled teachers, dorm counselors and administrative staff who were totally tuned in to adolescent needs and issues, and a cadre of students who were as interested in and capable of learning as she. What a mind-blowing experience! ...After (two more summers of) ... building on her previous experiences and continuing friendships ... she'll go off to college next year with confidence in herself and her skills, and a series of very successful 'mini-college' experiences to bolster her.*

Before discussing the values of summer residency programs, we must dispel three misconceptions that often negatively influence the early decision-making process about attendance at such programs, thus closing doors to summer opportunities for bright students. As the above testimonial may suggest, and the testimonials to follow will confirm, summer residency programs are not frills; they have brought about pivotal changes for many bright students and could play pivotal roles in the lives of many more teens.

1. Misconception: Parent says, "*Academic summer programs are only for the very brightest, and although my child is bright, she is not that bright.*" School personnel should take a proactive stance in correcting this viewpoint which is usually based on parents' lack of information. Guidance counselors, teachers and principals can help parents find a fit for the specific talents and interests of all bright students by reviewing a few periodicals that list summer academic options across the country. (See Appendix A.) Enrichment-based programs may use admissions criteria based largely on interest and/or minimal academic standards.

For example, teacher recommendations verifying that the student is above grade level in the particular area of study and student essays communicating interest in specific classes are common selectors. Even highly accelerative programs admit more than just the very brightest students. For example, programs based on the Talent Search model require applicants to score above the mean for college-bound seniors on the SAT or ACT. Of the approximately 150,000 7th and 8th grade students who annually test through this program, more than 20% (or 30,000) achieve scores this high. From this, we can estimate that because most of the programs serve 7th through 12th graders, 100,000 or more students from across the United States might be eligible in any given year. Your child may be one of these individuals. Parents of bright children need to know that programs vary in content and structure, but that most likely a program that fits a particular child's needs is out there.

2. Misconception: *Student says, "Academic programs are for nerds and dweebs, and I'm not going to any nerd camp."* Although information alone may help to dispel the parent version of this misconception, the child version is often much more firmly ingrained and difficult to overcome. Because our society has made it uncool to be smart or to be a high achiever, students often not only hide their talents in school, they resist associating with others they think their popular peers would consider unpopular. Even though they really may like to debate serious issues, think in more depth and excel in the classroom, they try to convince themselves that people like that are "not my type." Parents need to ease their highly capable yet reluctant learners into challenging summer programs. Unfortunately, there is no magic formula for accomplishing this; neither schools nor parents can or should push bright children into academic settings. The question is, according to one parent, how to "coax" without pushing.

The good news is that once the student has been "coaxed" and then has had the time of her life at an academic summer program, she becomes the best spokesperson in the world. Parents can provide their children with such students' testimonials, as well as accurate information, in order to change preconceived notions about "nerd camps." The best influence is a good friend of your child. Word-of-mouth probably brings more children to academic programs than any other vehicle. Even if there is no best friend to provide such influence, the buddy system often works, with several parents joining together to encourage their children to attend. Specific programs often have video tapes for distribution which will encourage young people to get involved. If students who look normal, and even cool, are shown having fun at something of interest or with an instructor who appears exciting, this may provide the impetus for your child to attend.

Because the uncool perception of scholarly nerds has become pervasive in our society, there are many bright children trapped by this misconception. However, some schools are working wholeheartedly to counteract anti-intellectual attitudes. The parents' job of coaxing will be easier if their school is one in which academic achievement is honored and encouraged — not just on paper, but through actions. This means, at the very least, that the school recognizes and rewards academic competition and achievement as enthusiastically and actively as it does athletic achievement. Parents will more easily find support if the school has a rigorous curriculum and school board-approved policies, such as those discussed in Chapter 3, whereby bright students can receive placement, credit and the opportunity for early graduation based on coursework taken during the summer.

3. Misconception: *Summer programs are for the rich, and we certainly can't afford them.* There are three levels of this misconception to be examined here. First, at the school level, personnel who could be opening doors to summer opportunities often start with the assumption that most of the children in their school will not be able to manage the financial commitment. Although often untrue, this is a logical assumption in any school that does not primarily serve the affluent. Consequently, school staff often fail to pass pertinent information on to their qualified students or, worse, they actively discourage students and parents from looking at summer program options. It is critical that school personnel be aware that financial support can usually be found for those who need it. They should explore multiple avenues of funding and help parents do the same. Many programs have generous scholarship and/or financial aid options for economically disadvantaged children, and in some, partial support is available to middle-class families. Eligibility for financial support varies greatly from program to program, so it pays to check out eligibility criteria before dismissing a program option. Because schools often offer a greater level of credibility than parents working in isolation, as institutions they should pursue financial support for student attendance at academic programs within their own business and service communities. As stated previously, business communities are often very willing to pay for a local student to attend a program.

Second, parents should always seek support before dismissing an opportunity. The more disadvantaged the parent is economically, the greater the chances that significant financial aid is somewhere to be found. But, as stated earlier, middle-class parents may also discover that generous support is available. *Generous* does not usually amount to full support, so middle class parents, like their more affluent neighbors, often have a value judgment to make: is sending our child to an academic summer program a worthy investment? Budgets may be pinched, but it might be the most important decision parents can make for their bright child.

Exploring your financial options may include such avenues as filling out forms revealing your family's financial status or spending time on the phone to seek out potential donors. Often, help is there for the asking. Also, look at academic summer programs as an investment in your child's future. As father of the many Talent Search-based summer programs around the country, Julian Stanley (1994) entreats, "Above all, don't view academic summer programs as expensive fun and games, frosting on the educational cake. They can be the most important ingredient. These and other things that give (your children) a cumulative educational advantage are likely to be the best *investments* in (their) education (you) could possibly make" (p. 4).

Third, students themselves can be very effective fund-raisers but, like their parents, they need to believe that they are making a sound investment. Some middle and high school students earn most or all of their summer program tuition. These are obviously not the reluctant, first-time participants. One of the financial issues for students is whether to earn money for this or another purpose. Students who become hooked on the value of summer residency programs during their pre- or early teens are most likely to become true believers in the value of working for the opportunity to attend such a program again. Those who are near the end of their high school careers are more apt to say they need to work *instead* of going to a summer program. If their reluctance is based on pop culture, including the desire to buy clothes, cars and stereos as well as remain cool, it may be next to impossible to convince them they are missing an important opportunity. However, if their reluctance is based on the need to save for college, there are two arguments that may convince them they can afford a summer program. First, if the program will earn them college credit, as many programs for older teens do, this may be worth more to them than money in the bank. Second, if they plan well, they may be able to "have their cake and eat it, too;" if a program takes up only part of their summer, they may be able to work as well.

The Value of Summer Programs — Parent and Student Voices

As mentioned in the previous chapter, academic summer programs include commuter as well as residential programs. Commuter programs cost less than residential ones and usually provide enrichment classes rather than accelerated course work, although some accelerative commuter programs do exist. They often provide for an introduction to a variety of new and different subjects and allow students to remain involved in other local summer activities. Parents of younger preteens, ages 10 and 11, may find that these benefits outweigh those of residential programs. However, one parent whose 11 year old had been to both types of programs reports, "Both commuter and residential programs are good for the talented child of this age, but the residential program is unique. It offers the kids opportunities to develop socially and emotionally through close contacts with peers and staff that day programs do not offer." Other parents who have sent their young preteens to both kinds of programs concur, and all emphasize the social benefits of residential programs. One parent adds, "Even though they (commuter programs) put less of a strain on your finances, they put more of a strain on parents' time when you consider driving the children, waiting for them or even the time it takes to arrange for alternatives like car pools." Our conclusion is that commuter programs are good, but residential programs add more dimensions for growth.

Interactions with hundreds of very bright students who have attended quality residential programs have convinced us that the benefits are greater in scope and influence than most are able to realize from reading either a single testimonial or a research study. These benefits exemplify the fit between student and curriculum, which we have previously described as the optimal match: rigor and pace meeting students' needs. But optimal match in this situation comes from more than just the curriculum; the social and emotional experiences of the residency program blend with the learning situation to compound its meaning. Students thrive when being smart is the common denominator. They frequently mention that because everyone is smart, the word or concept of intelligence never comes up. They are with true peers and, consequently, can just be themselves. Academic challenge, then, is one of many benefits of the summer program experience. Summer residency programs open many doors to the future. The parent and student voices that follow communicate what some of these doors might be.

One parent recently wrote, "(Our daughter) has been accepted at a top university for the fall semester. As you can see by her resume, she had a very impressive high school career. But the resume doesn't tell her whole story. The summer (residential) program showed her a whole different educational attitude and environment, and that made all the difference in her high school, college and life goals." Another writes, "(Our son) has investigated various (public) high schools in (our city), and has selected the one he feels will be most appropriate for him in terms of its challenging curriculum and highly motivated student body. We agree with his assessment and are submitting an application for transfer into that school. Before the summer (residential) experience, we doubt (our son) would have even considered, much less pursued, this possibility." And a third parent elaborates, "On the surface, one could say that (the accelerated summer residency program) is about presenting enriched academic subject matter at a pace that strives to match the breadth, depth and rate of the students' learning styles. But it is so much more. These initiating experiences gave my son (who is now finishing college) the self-confidence to be academically deep and broad. (He) speaks of the importance of 'nurturing his spark.'"

Paula Olszewski-Kubilius (1989), director and major researcher of Northwestern University's summer programs, would agree with these parent assessments. She outlined 14 ways in which summer programs positively influence the development of academic talent. These benefits are: challenging course work, self-testing of abilities, self-paced programs, intellectual peer interaction, social peer interaction, independent living skills, athletic activities, special counseling, environment for greater risk-taking, extracurricular activities, social networking, college exposure, educational opportunities and insight into self (pp. 224-226). Two other benefits reported in the literature and discussed by Olszewski-Kubilius should be added to the list: exposure to master teachers and continuous progress within an area of strength.

Premises

The above 16 values of summer programs can be condensed into three areas of development: academic, social and emotional. From collective data of summer program research, evaluation questionnaires and surveys, along with letters, interviews and informal conversations with students and parents, we have established the following premises about academic, social and emotional development through summer residency programs:

• A summer residency program and its participants must create an *optimal match* in order for maximum academic, social and optional benefits to occur for each student.
• Summer residency programs can and do have a profound influence on the social and emotional development of talented teens.
• Academic advantages of summer residency programs need to

be viewed from the perspective of significant long-term as well as short-term gains.

What follows is a discussion of the three specific developmental categories mentioned above, presented within the broader framework of Olszewski-Kubilius' many benefits.

Academic

Challenging or rigorous course work should be the bottom line if you are considering an academic program for your bright, brighter or brightest child. For any program, examine the appropriateness of the curriculum to your child's specific abilities, interests and learning needs before you begin seeking more detailed program information.

Many academic programs are located on college and university campuses, and many bright students like the early exposure to college life. One student states, "I was afraid that my high school was not preparing me for college. Here you get to see what college is like. You get to see the college students. You find out what it's like to have RAs (residential assistants) and TAs (teaching assistants) and roommates, and you find out what the work is like." Even if the programs are for younger students and the college students are not on campus during the time of the program, the stimulation of campus grounds and facilities (science laboratories, computer labs, libraries, dormitories, etc.) can make an impression that will increase interest in learning.

Often a summer program becomes the springboard to many other experiences. Instructors frequently become mentors and guide students through professional and personal connections that extend months or years beyond the initial experience. As an example, one instructor, a high school English teacher, is preparing a new accelerated literature and writing course for next summer. He invited two of the best writers from his past two summers of teaching to spend one week with him helping to define and prepare the new curriculum. During the same week he provided them with a mentorship in which they continued, shared and further developed their own writing skills. Another instructor, a college mathematics professor, invited three of his exceptionally talented mathematics students from the summer program, a high school freshman, sophomore and junior, to participate in a research project he was conducting on the randomness of quadratic residues.

As with the boy who was choosing a high school, students themselves become more aware of educational adventure and seek out more elusive academic options. Many simply better utilize the resources of their schools, while others go beyond that.

They call universities and make connections with people who can help them. They use their libraries, their phones, their computer networks and any other resources they can think of in finding the next step for themselves. And if they thought money was a deterrent before, they no longer do. If they want and find an option, they pursue it doggedly, including the means to pay for it.

One summer residency instructor said, "I want to pass on passion!" Good or challenging curriculum is predicated upon good instructors, experts who know their subjects, love their work and want to pass on their enthusiasm for their fields. There are master teachers in the schools, but the chances of your children working with them, as well as with equally able and motivated peers, are probably greater at a good summer program than through a public or private school.

Many students in summer programs note that contact with like-minded peers is the most important aspect of their academic experience. As one parent explains, "At the summer program (our daughter) immediately gets in touch with her intellect, is stimulated by the other students, and enjoys reading, writing and talking about deep, lifelong issues. She comes home looking and talking very passionately. It affords us as parents an opportunity to share some of our values that she is at other times not open to." Another parent comments, "In our small school it was difficult for our daughter to find friends who had similar interests. At some of the summer programs, particularly this one, she was able to socialize easily — to realize that she was not so different." A third parent sums up the message that most parents want to communicate regarding intellectual-peer interaction, "They sense that they are not the only one, but one of *many*. They find a sense of community with other talented individuals who are curious and who value learning."

Programs do vary in quality. As you are inquiring about the challenge of any program, you can get a feel for quality by asking about the background of the staff, the philosophy of the program and the level of all the classes, even if your child will be taking only one. If the program has been in existence for some time there may be objective data you can obtain, and you might ask for references. The best way to discover the reputation of a program is to talk to other parents whose children have been involved. An interesting question to ask the program director is, "How many students return to the program if they have that option?" Other questions might be, "How do you find your teachers? How do your courses compare to high school curriculum? Is there homework, and why or why not?" We suggest that you brainstorm a list of questions that concern you. These will vary depending on the age and maturity, strengths and weaknesses, and interests and motivations of your child.

Although current literature abounds with discussion of optimal-match curricula, the idea of optimal match between students is addressed less often. A significant criterion of accelerated programs is the selection process, which guarantees that the students will be with intellectual peers. In the words of one student, "I really had some problems academically at school because many of my peers were 'shallow' and (therefore) I didn't want to study. When I came here I was with *very smart* people and I learned that I can be smart too." Another student relates, "This experience has mainly made me work harder than I usually do. It showed me that there's a lot of competition out there, and that I need to stay on top of things." A third student says, "I have decided that many people in the world are very driven in their ambitions, and that they'll work very hard to gain advantages they feel are important. Before this I thought I was the only one possessing the aforementioned qualities. Because of my new knowledge (of other bright students), I will be even more directed toward my goals."

To summarize the academic benefits of summer residency programs, we return to our first premise: *A summer residency program and its participants must create an optimal match in order for maximum academic, social and emotional benefits to occur for each student.* This means that the program must provide an academic fit or appropriate challenge for your child and for all the other children in attendance. "The material presented should be a little too hard," exhorts one student. This suggestion parallels Feldhusen's (1995) definition of a curriculum commensurate with students' achievements: "The gist of academic challenge is that new tasks to be learned are just a bit beyond what the student already knows or has mastered" (p. 1).

Regarding the academic fit between participants, a student explains, "The best class I ever had was my writing class at (an accelerated summer program). Everyone in the class was a writer. Being with others who loved writing the way I did provided a kind of stimulation that just couldn't be experienced in any other way." Another student elaborates, "I had the opportunity to spend three weeks with kids who seemed like a different species from the kids I'd known before. These students want to learn; they're willing to help themselves to knowledge. They were curious about their chosen subjects and looked forward to class each day. At the end of each day it was common to hear excited chatter about the upcoming day's classes."

Social

One student explained what many students in accelerated programs feel, "*Everything* is equivalent to one year of school in three weeks, not just classes. Where it takes you 10 days to make a friend back home, you make friends in a few hours here. Everybody can communicate on a higher level, so amazing conversations take place. Whereas at school you may be depressed or down for 10 to 15 days in the course of a year, here it's one day and it's over. After leaving, you feel like you spent a year with the people in the program. It seems like the friends I've made in the last two years have been my friends for life!"

As we see here, it is difficult to isolate intellectual-peer from social-peer interaction at a quality summer residency program. They become one and the same. Silverman (1992) distinguishes between socialization and social development. Whereas socialization is the pressure to conform or adapt to the needs of the group, social development is a deep, comfortable level of self-acceptance that leads to true friendships with others. Individuals with good social development feel good about themselves, like other people, demonstrate concern for humanity and develop mutually rewarding relationships.

When we talk about making an investment in your child's future through summer programs, the academic investment is only the beginning; it is a social investment as well. Parents express the social benefits very simply. One reports, "My child developed comfort with himself socially." A second states, "I may never be able to use my phone again." Yet another says, "The social aspect has helped both my kids tremendously. As small children, they saw many of their peers as dumb jocks or goof-offs, quite rightly I fear. They felt rather isolated. Now they feel a part of a community rather than 'out-of-it!'" A fourth parent explains, "He developed a lot of friendships, something he doesn't easily do." And finally, a parent summarizes by saying, "Each year is better than the one before. He is more open with peers at this program, and is now extending himself more academically and socially back at home. There's a definite carry-over. We see that he's more confident, more aware that he needs more than the mainstream."

Obviously intellectual like-mindedness, a factor that is impeded by age, grade and heterogeneous groupings in school, leads to social development. Although the previous parent perspectives are clearly a reflection of what their children are telling them, more student comments add different ways of looking at the social element. One student reports, "I made some really good friends and gained a lot of confidence — which will help me make more new friends. Also, I think I'll be more selective about who to be friends with now." A second adds, "I was blown away by the compassion people here had compared to at home." Two sisters explain, "Though the classes were the main reason we came to the summer program, the social aspects were a definite bonus. It was stated in the program brochure and many speeches by attendants of the camp in years past that lifelong friends are made during the three weeks. Though it sounded impossible, the friendships we forged while at the program are probably stronger than the bonds we have with people we've known for years. Part of the reason we got along so well with these people was that we share common interests, hobbies and, of course, intellect."

Another student gives a slightly different slant to the social issue. He says, "I was waiting the whole year to come back, but when I did come back it was different. I suppose it will always be changing. I didn't make many new friends again, but I was at least one of the crowd." This exceptionally bright student had experienced synchrony (rather than asynchrony) during his first summer experience. His social self-concept as he returned the second year was considerably higher than it had been the first. The fact that he was "one of the crowd" indicates he had found some true peers and that many new friends, perhaps, were not necessary to his healthy social development.

Whether from cities, suburbs, small towns or rural communities, students express a need to see each other more than once a year. Rural students, especially, find it gratifying to meet during school holidays and breaks. As one student explains, "I'm teased and ostracized quite a bit at home. It's lonely. I really have nothing in common with the other kids, so I sit home a lot. But now I go to reunions with my (summer program) friends who care about education, have intelligent conversations and have goals for their future. We are kindred spirits. After not seeing your friends for months at a time, as soon as you see them there's no hesitation. You can just pick up where you left off, talking about war, religion, racial discrimination and other serious topics, intermixed with just silly conversation."

When asked about this social networking, one parent discussed the issue of geographical proximity between a program and a student's home. He said, "Although my older son (who traveled across the country to find the right program) made friends who made him aware that he was not alone, logistical limitations made the experience always a somewhat 'distant thing.' My younger son (who attended an equally challenging program in-state) says, "If I was so far away that I couldn't be in touch with my friends, (the summer program) would only be a memory for me. (The program) is much more than just a memory, it's part of my *real* life." Proximity does not mean within commuting distance; as these are residential programs, they need not be that close. Proximity does mean that most participants live within one to five hours or an easy day's driving distance from each other.

Although all students at academic programs should be very alike in their abilities (more true in accelerated than in enrichment programs), the students will and should be very diverse in their ethnic, environmental and economic backgrounds. Two instructors speak about the importance of talent coupled with diversity. One explains, "The fact that more than half of the students (in this program) have received vital financial aid has made a real difference in the classroom and campus atmosphere. It is unique — a socially and geographically diverse group of young people bonded together by an enthusiasm about learning." The second elaborates, "There's a range of abilities, albeit at the top end of the scale. There certainly is a range of individualities. Much may be made of the diverse composition of the student body. I am happy to report that ethnic and economic differences become irrelevant because what we're dealing with here are children of high to prodigious ability who are handicapped by their intelligence. I'm exhilarated because I've had the opportunity to teach some of the best students I've ever known."

Parents also share the advantages of a program that focuses on academic homogeneity, but diversity in every other respect. One parent explains, "This was the first chance my child has had to interact with a group of her intellectual peers. She now knows that amongst these peers her color, religion and economic level don't matter. Her self-esteem has increased greatly and she no longer feels that she's somehow different from the rest of the human race." A mother whose son became very close friends with a child of a different race and economic background writes, "I am haunted by thoughts of my son and his roommate, their similarities and their differences. There are thousands of kids like them who represent the brightest hope this country has for its future. Yet some of them will not make it. Saving one kid is probably like trying to empty the ocean with a paper cup. But that is no reason for us not to at least try. I realize now, as I really did not understand before, the tremendous importance of having such program(s) available to every (bright, brighter and brightest) child."

Emotional
Emotional growth occurs in children when basic health,

learning, love and friendship needs are being met. The beginning of emotional growth at summer programs lies with the development of self-confidence. Students speak of their changing views of their abilities: "When you're sitting in school, not being challenged, you start to lose faith in yourself and in your intellectual abilities. You start thinking, 'Maybe I'm not as smart as everyone thinks.' My class has made me more confident in my critical thinking skills. Coming here and pushing your limits is like a healing experience," says one. Another adds, "I always thought of myself as a 'math and science' person, but in this class I learned that I have great capabilities as a writer." A third joins in by saying, "This program totally turned my life around. Before coming I was so shy I would stay home and sleep all summer. I didn't think I was smart enough to be here. I wouldn't push my limits. I still don't know what my limits are, but I do know they are way far off. This gives me lots more self-confidence. In fact, it changed my approach to college. I'm applying to selective colleges that I would never have considered before."

Parents echo the students' statements. "She found that she belongs with the best students in the state and that she can succeed at work far beyond her typical school work," writes one. A second adds, "He's learned he can work through difficult problems." And a third parent points out, "My son often underestimated himself in the past. He now seems more self-assured, more willing to voice his opinion or disagree with a situation."

Self-awareness, self-insight and self-esteem are terms that indicate a deeper understanding of oneself. Building upon self-confidence as it relates to something specific, like academic successes or burgeoning friendships, self-esteem implies an appreciation and love of the whole self. Referring to self-awareness, one student explains, "This experience helped me to center on myself. When I'm writing a paper, I find myself searching for and writing much deeper meanings." A parent discusses her child's growth in self-insight: "I'm quite sure that having an experience on a college campus with a higher level of students has helped my son realize his knowledge and ability are not as great as he thought. Time spent in a more homogeneous group was very good for him." Another parent ties together her child's self confidence and self-esteem when saying, "She views herself differently and is more mature. Before, I would try to open doors and she would hesitate to even peek through. Now she's finding and opening her own doors."

Parents often struggle with the idea of letting their children go — in the sense of parting with them for a few weeks and in the sense of observing them becoming their own persons with different ideas. Yet the development of independence, the ability to live away from their parents and siblings while maintaining their sense of family identity, is one of the primary benefits of residency experiences. One parent expresses his hesitation in letting his daughter grapple with ideas foreign to her family culture, yet of his decision to let her go he says: "As our daughter grows and goes into the world, I realize she will be exposed to widely differing philosophies and beliefs. Part of her maturation will be to make choices and evaluate her experiences. Another part of her growing up will include my growing up as well.... We'll encourage her to attend next year. The program was very positive from both scholastic and social perspectives. It helped her self-esteem as well. Summer school with your program left us with a mixture of emotions." Another parent speaks of combined pain and joy after the program through a poem he wrote:

> *Letting go... I didn't know,*
> *Can't figure where the years did go.*
> *"It's a boy!" The sweetest joy,*
> *Could all of this have been God's ploy?*
> *"He's a man!" Now what's my plan?*
> *Can't find the bridge. I'm hurting... damn!*
> *Miss his need. 'Tis parents' greed,*
> *To hold the spirit that's been freed.*
> *Letting go... I didn't know,*
> *Can't figure where the years did go!*
> *(I hope it doesn't show.)*
> (Peters, 1994, p. 4)

Whether it is as simple as learning to separate their laundry (be prepared for tinted underwear if they are not prepared for this task ahead of time), or as complex as learning to live with a roommate, students learn independent-living skills that will make the transition into college and adult life smoother. Another parent reports, "I'm very proud of him and his accomplishments, and am both happy and sad to feel him moving away and into the real world. I do realize this is something which must happen. However, it's come sooner than I expected."

To summarize the social and emotional benefits of summer residency programs, we return to our second premise: *Summer residency programs can and do have a profound influence on the social and emotional development of talented teens.* Whether students attend just one program, as many do, or attend year after year because their love of learning and the social bonds literally drive them back, the whole is greater than the sum of the parts. These programs demonstrate that self-esteem does not occur in a vacuum; it is developed when students feel proud of having accomplished something that was difficult. Sometimes reaching for challenging goals means experiencing less than perfection. Examples include getting less than an A, not understanding part of a concept or producing less than was originally intended. Students who *fail* at a task at a young age often have an easier transition to college and adult life. As one student explained, "Now I know how much I can push myself. Knowing that there are others who are as smart and even smarter than me has helped me to know I can make mistakes and the world won't end. And I no longer feel a need to hide my intelligence in order to make friends." As we have seen, students inescapably grow as individuals, and they will not leave that growth behind when they return to their schools and communities.

We hope that this chapter has helped you to see the value of summer programs as stated in our third premise: *Academic advantages of summer residency programs need to be viewed from the perspective of significant long-term gains as well as from the short-term gains.* Many students consciously connect their experiences back to their middle and high school plans, their college-admissions preparations, and moreover, their lifelong pursuits. We will take a closer look at these connections in the last two chapters. Our goals will have been met if, through this chapter, just one more parent or one more teacher helps a child become part of a program that will significantly influence her life.

6-Cumulative Effects: The Whole Is Greater than the Sum of the Parts

If you have a 6th- or 7th-grade student, it may seem like a long journey to the 12th grade. Reading the previous chapters, you may think that there is plenty of time to consider extra-programming, to talk about career choices and to do long-term planning. But, just as it seems it was only yesterday when you watched him get on the bus for his first day in kindergarten, so will the teen years flash by. The investments you make today will begin paying off immediately for your child, while at the same time begin building his opportunities for the future.

Throughout this book, we have shared ways for you to help your child develop his talent. By paying attention to talent indicators, you can begin to determine if he is bright, brighter or brightest. All bright children need opportunities both in and out of the school setting for appropriate challenge. The level of rigor in his curriculum and his learning pace always need to match his level of growth and development, and therefore may change many times over the years. Enrichment and acceleration are both viable options, and which learning path is better at any given time can best be decided if you have a long-range plan. Such plans should include a school course schedule through grade 12 (taking into consideration the possibility of early graduation), as well as any enrichment classes and accelerated programs apart from the school setting and/or during the summer. Diagnostic-prescriptive assessment should be used to continually refine and update this plan. Striving for an optimal match of learning is the ideal. All students, including those of advanced intellect, should have the opportunity to progress in their learning through every class, every semester and every year. All students should receive credit and be placed appropriately based on what they already know. For example, it is punitive to put a student in beginning Spanish if he already knows that material, even if it has been learned outside the school setting.

None of the individual processes and ideas so far discussed occur in a vacuum. They build upon and work with each other to provide your child with what are called *cumulative effects* (Stanley, 1994). This can be likened to a birthday cake: Although the separate ingredients have individual nutritional benefits and different degrees of palatability, the end product of a special dessert is the true reward. Your child will digest all that is done to and for him, all of which will be absorbed and assimilated into his total growth and development. Knowing that his parents attempted to understand his needs and worked to meet them is a positive force that will help to move him into the adult world.

Ideas for a type of school that accommodates our bright to brightest students were presented in the pyramid model in Chapter 3. These ideas are validated in the following description:

Let us imagine schools whose purpose is to engage the intellect and to nourish the drive to mastery. Let us imagine schools which recognize that all students can attain excellence, but that not all students will master the same concepts and skills at the same time or in the same manner. Let us imagine schools that are flexible enough to accommodate individual differences, and brave enough to celebrate them. Let us imagine schools which teach children the value of social interaction, cooperation and community, but let us also imagine schools which encourage healthy competition, which reward individual initiative, which recognize that equity and excellence are not mutually exclusive — that it is in fact absurd to speak of one in the absence of the other.

(Durden & Tangherlini, 1993, p. 269)

We cannot ignore the fact that it is teachers who are given the delicate task of implementing these ideas. Csikszentmihalyi, Rathunde & Whalen (1993) present three major characteristics of influential teachers:

1. Memorable teachers are interesting in their own right. They "challenge students to expect more than just recognition or a paycheck from the work they choose. ...(This) inspires students to reconsider the intrinsic rewards of exploring a domain of knowledge" (p. 184).

2. Influential teachers can focus students' attention with "problems that pique curiosity and mobilize the skills of receptive learners. Such optimal conditions afford the close, well-paced match between task complexities and individual skills that is the hallmark of the flow experience" (p. 185).

3. They possess the "...unusual ability to perceive the emerging needs of often insecure young (gifted) people" (p. 188).

These characteristics are summed up in saying, " ...we cannot expect our children to become truly educated until we ensure that teachers know not only how to provide information but also how to spark the joy of learning" (p. 195).

We are a long way from realizing these ideals. Even if this type of school was available and these types of teachers were present in the numbers necessary, there would still be the need for continued learning outside the classroom. One bright dyslexic student who entered college early commented, "Every daily experience is a learning experience." This is an interesting way to look at the parent advocacy role as well. It takes time, money, perseverance and the willingness to do your own homework in understanding the issues to bring about important learning opportunities for your children. And every advocacy experience will be a learning experience for you, the parent.

By implementing the steps we propose, we do not guarantee you will understand your teenager or even always agree with him. After all, he is a teenager. But this book can help you be that guide-on-the-side as he learns how to learn, embraces learning as a lifelong opportunity and prepares himself for his future by working toward his potential. The explorations and experiences you provide for your child will both add to and subtract from his career choices, and this is good. An accelerated summer program student commented, "...As for my academic ambitions, I now know that there are really big challenges out there and I'm going to go out looking for them, not just in school, but in life too."

The remainder of this chapter will examine some additional parts of the talent development picture, bringing into focus how all the parts, with the help of the DEP (Differentiated Education Plan), will assist in moving your bright child toward a positive entrance into college. Let us first examine some further misconceptions.

Misconceptions

Three problems continue to emerge as parents struggle with issues of education for their bright children.

1. Misconception: *Whether my school says it has a gifted program or provides gifted programming, it still just separates my child out and makes him look different.* For many parents, separating who their child is from who they want him to be is a hard job. As parents, you must: 1) accept your child for who he is, 2) determine whether the school program will help your child or simply label him, and 3) guide your child into appropriate options based on your conclusions. Although we have made progress in the United States in appreciating and valuing diversity, there still is ambivalence when it comes to bright, brighter and brightest children. The 1993 government document *National Excellence: A Case for Developing America's Talent* states, "...A distrust of the intellect and an assumption that people should be allowed to develop to their full potential have clashed throughout American history and have muddled efforts to provide a quality education for the nation's most promising students. Today, exceptional talent is viewed as both a valuable human resource and a troublesome expression of eccentricity" (p, 13). Whatever your school does in gifted programming, it is more than separating him out. View it as a celebration of his differences and an attempt to maximize his potential.

2. Misconception: *If our school says my child is participating in gifted programming, then he should be going on field trips and bringing home neat stuff.* Good gifted programming need not be highly visible. The higher-level thinking skills and challenges can be blended into the curriculum so that some students may only learn the general facts, whereas other students use analysis, synthesis and evaluation to question facts and circumstances. This is an example of *differentiated learning.* Although this may work for our bright students and some of the brighter ones, it may still not be enough for the brightest. Acceleration in one or more subjects may be the *only* way to keep the brightest engaged in learning. As illustrated in Chapter 3, by the time students reach high school, there is enough difference in learning levels that it is important for our highly able students to have access to honors and Advanced Placement (AP) classes, as well as college coursework.

All students can benefit from field trips and extra, fun projects. All students, including the bright to brightest, have different learning styles, and learning is reinforced by different teaching approaches. If an activity is planned for bright students but does not meet the criteria of appropriate rigor and pace, then it should be offered to all students. To fail to do so leads to the misconception that working with our high potential students is elitist.

3. Misconception: *If an extra-programming experience does not directly change the school experience for my child, it will not make any difference.* Your child can benefit from extra-programming experiences, whether or not these experiences are formally acknowledged by his school and whether or not they change the content or pace of his school learning. Schools were never meant to be the only place of learning. However, it is advantageous for your child to keep records of all his experiences, whether or not they appear on his school transcript. He will use these records to demonstrate his interests, motivations and civic attitudes when filling out college application forms, seeking scholarship money and developing a resume. Extracurricular experiences do have an impact on post-secondary opportunities; any one of them could be the item that distinguishes your child as outstanding. Which experiences make that important impression will vary from institution to institution.

As discussed in Chapter 5, your child's attitude about himself and about learning can be markedly influenced through an out-of-school experience. This alone may stand as the most important reason for participation. One father reported that after his daughter's first year at a summer science camp, he noticed her increased confidence not only in science, but in general. She returned to the program three years in a row and told her father that those two weeks each summer kept her motivated throughout the year, even though her school was still "boring."

Advocacy
    Parents are, by nature of their position, their child's advocates. Some general guidelines may make your efforts more effective.
    All parents should view themselves as *partners* with the schools, not as adversaries, thus connecting with the schools in real and meaningful ways. For parents of the gifted, there are extra challenges. Your side of the partnership is strengthened by using your knowledge about your children. Consider the areas of optimal match, assessment, instructional rigor and achievement, self-esteem through achievement, and credit and placement wherever and whenever learning occurs, both within and outside the school system.
    Attaining an optimal match is often dependent upon good parent advocacy. Based on participation in science enrichment courses, one student was able to skip a general science course early in middle school, allowing him to take biology in 8th grade and leaving high school wide open for chemistry, physics and advanced science courses. A parent describes herself and her husband as "t & g gadflies" at their school. She reports that they will continue in that role of "talented and gifted" advocates because it has produced more success than failure. It is important for parents to realize that not every one of their efforts may be successful, but every little change may be significant.
    Helping our high-potential students requires parent education, assertiveness and perseverance. Reading this book is a good first step in educating yourself. Many of the titles in the *References and Resources* list can also help prepare you for the advocate role. Become familiar with your state statutes, school district policies and chain of command. Find a kindred spirit in the educational community to guide and help you through the maze and red tape. Keep a positive attitude and constantly remember that school personnel really do want to help your child, though their methods may be different from yours. One parent shared, "The school system would have discouraged our son from trying to excel. But two summers (of accelerated classes) helped us understand the importance of accelerating him and made us less afraid to tell the school what courses we feel are appropriate."

Above all, your teen needs to be the key player in his own life. His thoughts, ideas, opinions and beliefs must be addressed at every turn. Consider the following example. Two parents wanted help in planning their freshman daughter's three remaining high school years. They accompanied her to the guidance office and began talking with her counselor. Finally the girl interrupted, announcing that she had it all figured out. She wanted to finish high school by the end of her third year, go on a foreign exchange program to Japan for a school year and come back to graduate with her class. Her parents sat there amazed and asked why she had not told them this before. "You never asked!" she replied.

Connecting with the Schools

It is in your child's best interest to have any and all out-of-school activities incorporated when working with a DEP (Differentiated Education Plan). This means talking with school personnel on the DEP team, preferably well before prospective outside programs happen, about tying these opportunities into the regular school curriculum. The goal is to involve your child in systematic and continuous learning without unnecessary repetition. For example, if your son already knows basic computer programming skills and you have found a summer class in advanced computer programming, it would be a waste of time for him to take a normally required computer literacy class in the fall. Yet, be mindful of complexities in scheduling, along with a school's need for documentation. School personnel ultimately will want to be assured your child has learned what they consider necessary and important. Once they agree that he has adequate knowledge, scheduling a new course will take even more time and cooperation on their part.

Prior to a summer (or other) experience, the program brochure with the class description should be shared with the school. In this way the team can examine whether and how this class fits into your child's education. Will success in the class accelerate him into a higher level school class in the fall? Is there a "next" class to take there? Will high school credit be given? How much credit? Will there be a registered grade on his transcript? What kind of assessment information does the summer program instructor provide for you or the school to determine learning has occurred? Will your child need to take any other school tests to prove his knowledge and skills?

Many summer programs will provide documentation such as a course description, class syllabus and portfolio of work to define the class content compared to normal high school or college classes. Many will provide grades and suggestions for future courses. They may also supply, on request, supplemental information to help in making credit and placement decisions back at school. When choosing a summer experience, both parents and students need to look at the program's means of assessment and whether the program includes instructional rigor with potential for appropriate achievement and growth in self esteem.

If your school is not cooperative in working towards an appropriate DEP, this should not preclude extra programming. However, it may lead you and your child to some different and difficult choices. Perhaps summer classes can be taken that are not typically offered through your high school course sequence. Japanese or Russian language courses, for example, are much less commonly found in schools than Spanish or French and may be a good option to pursue in the summer. Taking classes that offer college credit benefits students after high school graduation. In some cases, a student might be excused from a series of lower-level classes in his home school to pursue more fitting curriculum through extra programming, such as accelerated mathematics.

The cost of these programs usually becomes a concern at this point. As previously discussed, in many instances there is money available and you need to consider how costs might be offset by decreased college costs. However, many parents have to bear the burden. Some states have legislation saying a school must pay for academic programs it cannot offer, so you need to become familiar with the laws and rules of your state. Do not expect to be told these facts by your school; research on your own part is usually necessary.

Assessment

The means to measure progress in learning is through assessment. Schools offer grades, standardized tests and parent conferences with verbal comments. These include the evaluation of behavior, attitude and skill development in addition to a measurement of new knowledge. Assessment is part of the diagnostic approach in the diagnostic-prescriptive model (see Chapter 3). Parents must recognize that all parts of assessment are like the many pieces to a puzzle. No single piece completes the picture. But each piece is a tool that will help you and your child form a meaningful plan in determining his future educational decision-making.

Understanding assessment subtleties is difficult at best. Teachers usually have autonomy in grading, and their biases can sneak in no matter how well defined and well-intentioned their process. Your questions about assessment may include: Is there a curve? Is grading standardized across grades and subjects? What are the criteria for grades? Are deportment and attendance a part of the grade, or does proof of knowledge stand alone? To help your child interpret grades, it is also important to examine other potentially significant factors. Girls may get higher marks for effort or good behavior. Boys may be marked down for unruliness, poor attitude or not turning in all required papers. Grades in difficult classes may carry the same weight in GPA's (grade point average) as grades in easy classes.

Many of our highly capable students are bored in school, and consequently they quit trying to succeed. In such cases, poor grades may not mean lack of knowledge. According to *National Excellence* (1993), recent studies show that gifted and talented elementary school students have mastered from 35-50% of the curriculum to be offered in five basic subjects before they begin the school year. Then a student has many months ahead of sitting in a classroom learning nothing new, yet being told he must pay attention. Imagine what that can do to attitude and self-esteem by the time students reach middle and high school. Good grades do not necessarily indicate learning is taking place, and grades other than A's do not always mean a student is doing poorly.

Grades should be based on knowledge gained through a student's clear understanding of learning objectives and pre-discussed criteria; that is, what the teacher expects for proof of learning. In assessing growth and learning, schools should separate knowledge and comprehension from acquired skills, attitude and behavior. For example, a student's final assessment may show that he mastered the curriculum at an A level, even though he was inattentive and disruptive during the class. The behavioral problem would not negatively affect his grade and result in his having to repeat curriculum that he actually knows very well. His poor attention needs to be recorded and he needs to correct it, but the record should be within the context of deportment rather than content mastery. Then he would receive his A and also know that he must modify his behavior in future learning situations.

Maintaining perfect grades is a constant concern of many high performing high school students. They fear their GPA will fall if they do not get A's in honors, Advanced Placement or college classes, or in other accelerated options in or out of the school setting. How will this affect entrance to college or potential scholarship money? Looking only at the GPA does not give very good information because, as explained, grading is neither standardized nor always based on subject proficiency. Here again comes a difficult decision for the student: "Do I deny myself the challenging opportunity for a special learning experience because I may not get an A, or do I take the risk and know that, ultimately, personal growth and learning are most important?" An option some schools offer is to take a class pass/fail with no grade issued. It is a reality that scholarship money is available for students with perfect or near-perfect grades. As part of the plan, students should inquire early about criteria for specific colleges and scholarships. They will also want to know how grades versus rigor are balanced in formulas for both college entrance and monetary considerations.

Two tests discussed earlier in the context of Talent Search are commonly used to screen college applicants: the American College Test (ACT) and the Scholastic Assessment Test (SAT). Colleges advertise which test they use, and students take the test for entrance to the college of their choice. Many take both tests, especially if they live in the Midwest, where the ACT is more prevalent. This would be our recommendation, because it gives your child the flexibility to apply to a variety of schools, from prestigious universities to specialty schools to the college near home to a school at which his acceptance is a certainty.

ETS (Educational Testing Service), the SAT agency, records and maintains all SAT scores acquired while a student is in grades 9-12. Once a student requests his SAT scores be sent for admission to a specific college, ETS will send **all** scores on record. Therefore, it might not be wise for a student to take the test once he is in high school until he is ready to begin the college application process. ACT scores, on the other hand, are only sent to colleges upon student request. So a student may take the ACT at any time during his high school years for practice or for purposes of entrance to precollege programs without fear of affecting his college entrance chances should he get lower scores during earlier testing attempts.

Although both the ACT and SAT testing services say that study for either college entrance exam is not necessary, study programs and classes abound. High ACT and SAT scores do make a difference in getting into colleges of choice and in getting merit awards. If your bright student is not a good test-taker or suffers from test anxiety, you might want to consider having him participate in a preparation program. Most bright students do not need these services, although we do recommend that they get experience with both tests early through participation in a Talent Search program. (See Appendix A for national Talent Search sites.)

The PSAT (Preliminary Scholastic Assessment Test) is administered by ETS in the fall of the junior year to college-bound students in their own high schools. Colleges commonly consider these scores for recruiting purposes, and PSAT scores are used for determination of finalists in the National Merit Scholarship competition. Colleges also often use PSAT scores for distribution of their own merit scholarships. In addition, many businesses throughout the country sponsor scholarships based on these scores. It is advantageous and possible for academically talented sophomores, and even freshmen, to take this test. It is good practice and gets top-scoring students on top-college recruiting lists early. Also, it provides flexibility if a student should decide he wants to graduate from high school early. However, please note these few words of caution: Students (under most circumstances) *must* retake the PSAT as juniors. Exceptions to this rule include the following:

1) If your child decides as a sophomore that he wishes to graduate at the end of his next year of school, he can notify ETS of his intention and ask that his sophomore scores be considered for National Merit.

2) If he decides during his junior year to graduate early after having taken the PSAT in the normal cycle, ETS should also be notified. He can still be considered for a National Merit Scholarship, but there will probably be a year delay.

3) If for some reason the PSAT cannot be taken during the junior year, sophomore scores will not be used even though they are available and would qualify the student for scholarship. For example, one boy took the PSAT during his sophomore year and scored in the National Merit semifinalist award range. He started receiving literature from all the most prestigious colleges in the country during the following summer. Then in the fall he was in a serious auto accident that kept him from retesting as a junior. His sophomore scores could not be used. With special consideration from ETS, this boy was allowed to substitute his junior-year SAT scores for National Merit purposes. Students need to be aware that such permission is only given when ETS considers the circumstances that have eliminated the possibility of legitimate junior-year PSAT testing.

Understanding and applying the many tools of assessment can help our highly able students to determine their future directions. However, do not forget that the constantly changing and growing child cannot continue to wear the same-size or even a one-size-fits-all educational shoe.

Credit and Placement

School credit should be granted upon documentation of proficiency in a subject, whether or not the class was formally taken and whether or not the student actually sat in a class for the full semester. In addition to common modes of assessment discussed earlier, documentation of proficiency can include a portfolio of work or products, high evaluation by a mentor or other professional, passing of the same final test given to students in the formal class or passing a type of standardized test. A grade may be given with the credit, or a pass/fail assessment may be applied. If a grade is given, the proficiency level expected by the school should be consistent with that expected of all students within the regular course structure; for example, if 92% defines an A in the equivalent school class, then 92% should define an A in an alternative situation. Likewise, if 92% defines an A in a 5-point course through a weighted-grade system and the student can demonstrate that he has completed an equally difficult or more rigorous course, a 5-point (rather than a 4-point) A should be awarded. Although weighted grades are supposed to equalize grading in difficult courses, often you will be faced with a punitive situation if a district does not have policy that allows for alternative courses to count as part of its weighted grade program. As stated previously, if at all possible you should discuss placement, credit and grade issues with the school as early as possible.

Placement may be considered along with or separately from the credit issue. In either case, placement should be consistent with ability and pace of learning. If a student has received a score of 520 or better on the math section of the SAT in a middle school Talent Search, he is ready for algebra immediately and a fast-paced math program which moves him quickly through four years of high school math. He could successfully finish at least a year of calculus before graduating from high school. A proficient middle-school writer who also has high verbal standardized scores on a national achievement test may be ready to take an upper-level high school writing class rather than 9th-grade English. Such students may have different motivations but still have options as to when they graduate from high school. "I'll be two years ahead in math," said one aspiring youth. "I want to earn scholarships to a good medical school, and this acceleration and program will look good on my applications."

The bottom line is that we should no longer be lock-stepped into a system in which a student must spend a set number of minutes in a specified class in order to earn credit or a grade before being able to move on in any area of learning.

Looking Ahead

A kindergartner may have an idea of what he wants to be when he grows up, but when he gets to those early teen years, things may begin to get fuzzy. An academically talented student's many abilities can confuse the issue. A female becomes aware that some things she likes do not meet with the approval of her peer group. A student with a single interest can vacillate from being sure of the goal to feeling trapped in a certain mold. A parent's difficult task is to guide the child through these trying years with one eye on today and the other on the future. Keep in mind that a bright student with special opportunities may very well be success-ful in a variety of careers. Parents should not seek just one option for that child, nor should they assume that a child cannot change careers.

Having an educational plan can be the impetus for serious discussion about college choices, majors in college and, ultimately, career paths. We are not suggesting that your child will know what he wants to become, but rather that his ideas for the future can begin to have some relationship to what he is doing today, even in middle school. Vocational projections suggest that students today will most likely have many jobs and probably more than one career path.

Although academically talented students usually do not have trouble getting into college, competition for certain colleges and specific courses of study is intense. Therefore, it is important to demonstrate individual assets in ways other than grades, test scores and advanced coursework in high school. Documentation of all extracurricular activities including jobs, volunteer activities, compe-titions, contests, research projects and courses or options taken during summers is crucial. Such documentation, in a cumulative portfolio or other means, demonstrates both depth and breadth in learning as well as creativity, motivation, cooperation and civic attitudes.

A student may face some hard choices between what may feel safe or easy versus what will create the most options after high school. You might want to share with your child the saying that it is not only your aptitude, but your attitude, that will determine your altitude. Looking for the day-to-day challenges and excite-ment of learning, and watching for those windows of opportunity, will benefit him today and in the future. The opportunities begin to spiral, and everything builds on everything else. One summer program student stated, "Before I came to (the summer program) this year, my interests for the future had nothing to do with diplo-macy or politics. Now, it's as if a whole new arena of options has unfolded before my eyes. Allowing no alternatives which tantalize [sic] my ambitions, I am fairly certain that the direction of my life will inevitably flow toward geopolitics." This was certainly an "aha!" experience for this student, yet she hedges to keep options open as she wonders what will come next.

7 - A Fit for All Academically Talented Teens

In considering gifted education, it is now time to let go of any stereotypical ideas. In the previous six chapters we have presented a fresh view of what talent development could be and who has talent. It is essential for all to remember that talent development is not elitist. Talent resides in children with no homes just as it does in those with comfortable houses to return to each day, and in children regardless of their skin color or ethnic backgrounds. Talent resides in teens from farms in rural America just as it does in their suburban counterparts, in the girl down the street as well as in the boy next door.

Although it is difficult to assure skeptics of gifted education that talent development includes individuals in all of the above groups, it is even more difficult to battle societal conditions that make talent development less accessible to some of these children than to others. Yet there are still other groups of children to consider when discussing the needs of bright children. These are youngsters whose talents are even less identifiable and even less easy to support once they are identified. We are talking, first, of children whose learning weaknesses become such a dominant force in their lives that their strengths or talents are overlooked, squelched, diminished and ultimately not developed even as they purportedly receive special educational services. Indeed, talent resides in children with learning disabilities such as dyslexia or attention deficit hyperactivity disorder (ADD or ADHD) just as it does in children who read at age 2 or 3. Second, we are talking about talented children labeled as under- or overachievers, those who achieve either less than they are capable of or who achieve at levels so high that it seems impossible. In fact, the spectrum of under/over achievement is unique in that it is the only case in which society fails to recognize talent on both ends. In truth, we believe that overachievement is a misnomer; a person cannot accomplish more than she is capable of accomplishing. Certainly, perfectionism is an issue with bright children, and some do try to accomplish more than is healthy for themselves. However, if a child is producing incredible results in any talent field, that talent is real.

Case Stories — Real Answers from Real Students

The following stories tell of four teens who have benefited from academic summer residency programs. These profiles represent students who, from an elitist perspective of gifted education, might not be viewed as typical participants in such programs. Unfortunately, they also represent students who are often overlooked in their schools. In sharing their real-life stories here, our purposes are threefold: (1) To clarify who these children are and that they do exist, (2) To show not only that summer programs can make a difference, but to suggest that any appropriate educational options through any institution would be equally important and (3) To demonstrate the significance of cumulative effects.

These children's stories must remain unfinished by definition. Two are still in high school and two are college freshmen; none is at an age at which we can even think about the final word regarding their talent development. But by peeking into their talent beginnings and their goals for the future, we can anticipate what might be the later whole of these cumulative effects.

Case Story #1 — Sally

Sally lives in what she calls "the boondocks." Her father used to run a dairy farm until he became ill and could no longer handle the demanding regimen. Now their farm land is rented out, Sally's father is attending college to become a math teacher and Sally's mother tries to hold the family's finances together on her salary as a special education teacher in the district where Sally attends school. Sally laments, "We all do many things to make money, but there never seems to be enough."

Sally's parents have always encouraged her to develop her creativity and to live up to her abilities. Both their farming and teaching backgrounds taught them that different children learn things at different paces and in different ways. Yet Sally says that even though she was always the smartest and her parents encouraged her interest in learning, she never thought of herself as talented or gifted until she was in the 7th grade. Then, through the encouragement of her counselor she took the SAT. She scored above the mean for high school seniors on both the verbal and math sections and was in a high enough percentile on the math portion to really take note. She remembers, "I read my math percentile and I thought, 'Wow! I'm only in 7th grade and I can do this?' It really boosts your self-esteem."

Sally does not hesitate to point out the disadvantages of living in a rural area. Her high school has a population of 80 and her graduating class has fewer than 20 students. She is perceived by her classmates as the perfect student. Because she always gets the answers right in school, and because she simply is not interested in small-town stuff, she does not fit the local teenage social scene. At her school there are fewer AP or honors options available than in other schools, as she is well aware, and they have not yet entered the technology age; distance learning is not an option. It is a drain on the family's time as well as their budget to seek out opportunities from greater distances, but they do.

Based on her excellent Talent Search scores and her need for opportunities beyond school, Sally's parents encouraged her to apply for a scholarship that would enable her to attend an academic summer residential program. She did receive the financial aid necessary to make the accelerated summer program (hereafter referred to as ASP) a reality. Sally says, "When I first got to ASP I thought, 'What am I doing here?' This was the first time I was not the smartest — I could actually learn from another student."

Sally contrasts being smart at her school to attending classes at ASP. "At school, math is my strong subject. I am accelerated three grades in math; to advance you through the grades is something they can do in a small school. But in math and everything else, I'm supposed to know everything; I'm not supposed to have questions. At ASP I took a course in Geopolitics, something really different! The course had me lost at first. You're reading above your level (college-level material) and half of the time you're wondering (of the instructor), 'What *is* he saying?' But it's just being exposed to new information that's great. Your instructors want you to try to figure things out. You learn that you can't know everything."

What about grades? For many of the students in rigorous summer programs, especially students who come from schools with fewer students with whom to compete and fewer advanced courses, there is that initial shock of finding out that you are not the only smart one and probably not the smartest; there is also the surprise at having to work hard for a good evaluation. Sally tells how she "hung in there" and discovered that she was actually grasping the new material quite rapidly. "My favorite story about my achievement is when I got 102% on an ASP exam. One of my friends started congratulating me, telling me *that's so good*, and telling everyone about it. That would never have happened in school. It made me realize that getting a good grade is really a good thing. I don't have to be ashamed about getting the highest score. I shouldn't coast through school. I got an A in the course, and just like my scores on the SAT, it has increased my self-esteem. This is the first time that someone I looked up to so much, someone who ordinarily teaches college students, gave me feedback that I was so good....Everyone did really well, although I know a couple of my friends didn't get A's. It was hard at first for them to accept less than the perfect evaluations they usually got. But I think they're also very proud of their accomplishments. It was a really hard course and they know that an A/B or a B here is worth a lot more than an A in an easy course back home. Also, they don't have to figure it into their high school GPA's if they don't want to."

What about friendships and going back to her small rural school? In Sally's words, "I have been reassured that there is life beyond high school." She regularly (two to three times a year) attends reunions with her ASP friends from around the state. She says it is enough to help her survive what they all call "PADS" — Post-ASP-Depression-Syndrome! And she has found new talents in both herself and her teachers back at school. She is acting at school and in community theater. Of her teachers she says, "I have found that I have some very supportive teachers. They really know me and my abilities. I've had quite a bit of personal attention. I think that's a big advantage of attending a small school — teachers really are willing to take you under their wings."

ASP, acting and supportive teachers back home have helped Sally set her sights high for the future. "I still like math and I'm still good at it. But I've decided I want to become a Broadway actress. Life, like math, was orderly and logical when I was little. But it changed. Now I see so many different possibilities." Sally sees her investment in ASP classes and excelling there as an important step toward getting into a good "liberal arts, private, expensive school." She knows she will have to get a good scholarship but knows also that her resume is looking better all the time. She has her accelerated summer work documented on her transcript and now also has completed an ASP course for college credit. Her acting and other extracurricular activities are impressive. And, although she is from a small school, her excellent school record and her outstanding test scores, now including the important PSAT, will serve her well. Regarding her need for financial support, she says, "I wouldn't have been able to attend ASP without it. Before I came to ASP, I thought that the world out there was getting meaner. But I've learned there are still people in this world with generosity, kindness and a will to help others. I have confidence that I can compete for college scholarships. And I hope someday I'll be able to help another child the way my sponsors have helped me."

Case Story #2 — Jared
Jared is African American and lives in the inner city with his mother and several siblings who seem to come and go on a regular basis. His father left home when he was little and was recently killed. Drugs and violence are part of his environment. Though none of his siblings has taken an interest in school, and all of his older siblings have dropped out, Jared has always loved learning and aimed for perfection. "Studying," he says, "is just something I do."

Like many bright students, Jared says he did not realize that he was talented until middle school. But then his reluctance to take academic risks began. He was fortunate, however, to have a special teacher who noticed that he was "cruising." With this teacher's personal guidance and persistence over a three-year period, he slowly became involved in more challenging curricular options. First she offered him extra-credit projects, and he resisted. He worried about doing anything harder, but his teacher insisted that he could do it. Next she suggested he participate in Talent Search, and again he resisted. His excuse this time was that he could not afford it, but his teacher got the school to pay for the test. Next she suggested that he attend ASP, and he resisted. Again he used money as an excuse, and again his teacher assured him that financial aid was available and she would help him apply for it. Jared explains, "I wasn't going to go to ASP, but I got a scholarship: tuition, room and board, transportation, books, spending money —everything! I was still going to back out because I didn't want to embarrass myself by being at the bottom of the class. I worry about being a failure to myself more than to anybody else. I usually put more pressure on myself than I have to. My mom tells me that's bad."

Jared speaks with quiet respect about his teachers, but

there is a special glow, a strong sense of pride when he talks about his mother. "My mom," he says, "is a very large part of my success. I can always turn to her. She's very wise. She encourages me to do things, which now I try to resist less often." He explains why he resists less, implying that resistance is still in his repertoire. "I've been to ASP for three summers now, and I have changed each year. The first year I stayed in my room and studied all the time because I didn't want to fail. I was surprised to learn I could do geometry in three weeks and get an A. The next summer I took a course in supercomputers. I pushed myself to participate in the activities more and found that there were other quiet kids like me. There's really a social group for everyone. The supercomputers course is what got me hooked on computers. I plan to pursue a career in computers. So this summer I applied all on my own to take another computer course, and I'm planning to take an ASP course for college credit next year."

So where is Jared's resistance these days? It still kicks in when the doors that open seem beyond his very focused education and career goals. Recently, two opportunities came his way; one did not fit his beliefs of what he could and should do, and the other did. At this point, his self-esteem and his knowledge of where he wants to go in life are strong enough that he can afford to resist a little. So, he declined the first option — an offer by the city Rotary Club to study through its foreign-exchange program in Chile, all expenses paid. "I just need to concentrate on school," he explains. The second option came through ASP, and he not only accepted it, he had to stretch himself up front to get it. His scholarship sponsor, a major corporation, offered him the possibility of summer employment in addition to support for his three weeks of study. He submitted a resume; he had never written one before. And he nervously but successfully completed his first job interview for something other than a part-time job at a fast-food restaurant. The experience gained on this job will be a valuable addition to his now-growing resume.

Jared says, "These programs help you a lot because they give you security and confidence. They assure you that you're talented as well as knowledgeable overall." After his first year at ASP he said he would not return if he could not maintain his GPA because, "I wouldn't be able to say that I belong with people like this." After three years in the program he says he has learned that there is a large diversity of students when it comes to talent. In this unique setting he feels he can ignore artificial social barriers and sample a variety of friendships that would not be possible at his own high school. "My career choice has remained the same for two years," he says, "but my philosophy of life has grown to include meeting as many new people as possible."

Regarding money, Jared says he still puts more pressure on himself when he is being supported by someone else's money. "But," he adds, "I think all students should feel that way about their parents' financial support too."

Jared's mother summarizes, "I live in the inner city and it's hard to raise children here with all that goes on, the gangs and so on. I've been blessed with a child who has no interest in what goes on in the streets. He has a great love for learning. It's the joy of his life. The more he learns, the more he wants to learn. He is a good son and has a great love for people. He will use his knowledge to help others."

Case Story #3 — Mark

Mark had always done well on tests and the one thing he loves — math. But that was as far as it went. He reported that at school he felt like "an odd-ball geek," and he had as much trouble making good friends as he did making good grades. His parents revealed that he had ADD, which medication helped him to control. Even so, he continued to be a very uneven student, getting one or two A's each semester and the rest D's and F's. If he did not care for a subject, he just did not do his homework. Everyone knew why his grades were poor, but they could not force him to finish his work. In fact, his counselor reported that Mark often claimed to have done the work but just failed to hand it in.

All that changed when he came to ASP. Mark started this new venture with what was safe — math. He took his medicine independently, and he had no choice but to study math more or less independently. He was in a self-paced math course in which students were expected to complete a year's worth of high school course work at their own direction, with the instructor acting as a guide-on-the-side. What surprised Mark, his parents and teachers back at his school was not that he did well in this course, as it was in his area of interest, but how well. He was responsible for setting his own pace. Mark may have Attention Deficit Disorder, but it was not noticed during the three weeks in which he completed two years of high school math.

His parents wrote, "This was the first time Mark ever had a math teacher who could answer his questions and relate to him. We think he has proved to himself, us and hopefully the school, that he can excel in spite of his ADD." This was three years ago, and Mark's scholastic life did not move in a straight line to the top. Yet neither did it fall to the bottom or come to a dead end. Rather, it spiraled him into a four-year university with knowledge that he can succeed and that it is his choice. He also knows that it will be easy to fall into the same old traps, especially as he will have to take many courses not of particular interest to him.

Of his own experiences, Mark says, "I've never had something that everyone seems to expect gifted kids to have — a high grade point average. Besides, a 2.5 GPA doesn't exactly impress college admissions officers. What got me into college was the chain-effect of some very definite events. First, I was recognized in Talent Search and that was a confidence-booster. Then I took that first ASP course in which I did so well. That taught me I could concentrate, even though I continued to goof off much of the time. Then I took the university-credit course through ASP here on this campus. I knew that I only got accepted by this university for that course because ASP gave me a letter of recommendation when my grades weren't good enough for admission. Before coming to that program, my occasional successes were like the warm-ups a runner does prior to a big race. All of a sudden I was ready for the race of my lifetime; I realized that this was where I wanted to go to college, not the two-year campus I was headed for. And I knew that I was going to have to work very hard in my senior year to get here. The number theory course I took here through ASP cemented my decision to major in applied mathematics."

We worry about Mark more than other students who have overcome obstacles to their talent development. He still has to fight, basically all on his own, to do what his courses at ASP got him to do. In his words, "Both were intense and challenging and forced me, out of a desire to survive, to do what my teachers have been trying to force me to do for four years — to work to my potential." We are not sure who will force him to do that now; we hope his will to survive includes four years of sometimes intense, but often less interesting, college work.

Case Story #4 — Mary
Mary is intellectually industrious. She was among the

brightest students at her school and among the brightest students at ASP. She is multifaceted, with abilities not only in the more academic areas of mathematics, science, writing and foreign languages, but also in the arts and athletics. She is a skilled painter, an accomplished violinist and a top runner on her school cross country team. She has pursued many facets of her learning through ASP, taking courses that have included engineering, Japanese language, chemistry and philosophy.

At ASP, girls appear no different, academically, from the boys; the problem is that starting in 7th grade and continuing through about 10th grade, there are many fewer girls in accelerated programs. We asked Mary why she thought girls were less apt to pursue outside opportunities than boys. She replied, "In the school setting, boys have self-confidence and girls don't. If a guy does well at something, everyone respects him; it can be academic as well as athletic. If girls do well in academics, it's considered different, and so to be smart is to be different. In junior high there's this quest for conformity for girls. It's kind of a *de facto* discrimination against girls. You see these cliques where everyone tries to be like everyone else. Girls tend to back away from their school work and talk about other things. They don't want to seem smart. For a girl, that's very hard in junior high."

When it is pointed out to Mary that she refers to girls by using the pronoun "they" almost as if she was not a part of the "girl group," she laughs and says, "I truthfully can't identify. I admit I've always preferred to work with boys rather than girls. They have a lot more self-confidence and a lot more focus when they go into a project, and you can be a lot more effective and get a lot more done."

What, then, encourages Mary to be different from other girls? She proclaims without hesitation that it is her family. Mary says that her parents were responsible for getting her into ASP, and that she thinks family is the most important ingredient in talent development. Given the clear messages she received at home from the time she was little that it was good to be curious and good to do different things, she never suffered from the desire to conform. "Because I have a strong family bond and I have so many people giving me help, I realize that to not have self-confidence is to not be happy. I love learning. To be successful at something makes me happy. I think girls need even more opportunities for challenge than boys. To go to a program like ASP is so important because people respect you for who you are, for your abilities; being smart isn't an issue."

Mary's very strong preference for working with boys as opposed to girls made us wonder how she felt about working with girls in ASP and at other special programs such as her youth symphony orchestra. She responded, "All the girls at ASP act more like the boys back at school in that we all want to do really well and we all know we have to do really well to accomplish our goals." That statement reinforces our observation that, from a scholastic or talent development standpoint, gender differences disappear when the setting provides an optimal match in curriculum and student body.

Mary is so self-confident, so in control, that we wonder if she is ever upset and if she has ever failed at anything. She explains, "I've had lots of doubts. I haven't always met my goals. But to fail only makes you try harder to be successful...I've cried many times. I remember a time when I wasn't invited to a party by my supposedly good friend. She didn't think the kids would want to be around someone who was smart; she wanted to impress the other people that she was cool. I remember another time sitting in the counselor's office with my mother, afraid I wouldn't be able to take a course that was important to me. But," Mary continues, "high school is much better for smart girls than junior high school because there are so many more activities that you can get involved in." For instance, Mary was on the newspaper staff and says she met students from other parts of the city that she would not have met otherwise. She explains that hanging out in the newspaper office from the time she was a freshman meant holding incredible conversations with people who were cool to her, boys as well as girls, seniors as well as classmates from lower grades. She admits that this might not work for girls going to small schools, but in her large city school, it worked for her.

Even though high school was good for Mary, she needed to go beyond school to reach her goals. On top of all her other advanced courses and extracurricular activities, she studied Japanese for college credit at a local college through the state's post-secondary-options provision. She also traveled to Japan twice, once with her ASP instructor and once through a foreign-exchange program. In addition to earning university credits through the school's Advanced Placement courses, she earned university credits in both philosophy and chemistry through the ASP program. She graduated from high school early and has started her first year of college at age 16 with enough banked credits to allow her to obtain a Bachelor's Degree in less than three years. She says, "I believe that ASP has provided me with preparation for going to college that I could have never received elsewhere. Every time I took a course it seemed like another possibility also opened up — like foreign travel and post-secondary options. At the same time it has given me a supportive social and intellectual network that will be a part of my life forever. It has helped me to feel proud to be me."

Conclusion

There is no question in our minds that teens with talent must have a wide array of challenging opportunities if their potential is to be developed. As we have mentioned, differences disappear when you bring like-minded students together in common pursuits, their differences melding into the wonderful commonality of shared passions. If our society expects little of teenagers, the majority will produce little. But if society expects more, there is no limit to what many of our teens will produce.

We asked a broad cross-section of talented teens to summarize the most important elements for parents and schools, if talent development were to become the norm. Here is what they said.

In School

In grades 5-8, schools should:
- encourage creativity
- encourage independent learning
- help smart kids not to feel alone
- make academics equally as important as sports
- eliminate the "nerd" attitude

In grades 9-12, schools should:
- provide more in-depth studies
- provide more advanced classes
- provide post-secondary options
- eliminate mainstreaming (inclusion)
- increase standards in essay writing and speaking
- encourage independent thinking
- encourage lifelong thinking

In all grades, schools should:
- respect students' learning abilities

- push students to reach their limits
- allow students to learn at their own paces

At Home
Parents of bright students, ages 10-13, should:
- let them be themselves at home
- help them through difficult times
- encourage them to explore many talents and learning options
- value creativity

Parents of bright students, ages 14-18, should:
- let them take charge and make their own mistakes
- be good role models
- encourage self-motivation
- help them channel their talents into accomplishments
- let them go

Parents of bright students of all ages should:
- be involved in schools
- campaign for rigorous programs
- support their children's activities
- teach the importance of having good vocabularies

As we write this book, there are many bright, brighter and brightest children out there who are not being challenged at all. In America, too many of our decision-makers are afraid of hurting someone if we say that a particular individual is very bright and something must be done about it. Because of this, all across the country the needs of many children are not being met.

The student voices in this chapter join the chorus of the many youngsters we have known. The message to their parents is, *You are the most important people in the world. Keep opening the doors for your bright children, just as our parents opened doors for us. It's not always easy, but it can be done.* To school and community leaders, their refrain is, *Parents can't do it alone. We need your help if there are to be many different kinds and levels of opportunities for talented teens. We may all be bright, brighter and brightest, but we are all different as well. We want to study different things and achieve happiness through pursuing different life goals. Your stewardship today in opening doors for us, helps create the future for many generations to come.*

PPENDIX A

gional Talent Search Sites

Center for Talent Development (CTD)
Northwestern University
617 Dartmouth Place
Evanston, IL 60208, 708-491-3782

Center for Talented Youth (CTY)
The Johns Hopkins University
3400 North Charles Street
Baltimore, MD 21218, 410-516-0337

Rocky Mountain Talent Search (RMTS)
University of Denver
Wesley Hall
2135 East Wesley
Denver, CO 80208, 303-871-2533

Talent Identification Program (TIP)
Duke University
Box 90747
Durham, NC 27708-0747, 919-684-3847

dditional Resources for Programming

Center for Gifted Education
College of William and Mary
Jones Hall Room 304
Williamsburg, VA 23185, 804-221-2362

Connie Belin National Center for Gifted Education
210 Lindquist Center
The University of Iowa
Iowa City, IA 52242, 319-335-6148, 1-800-336-6463

Education Program for Gifted Youth (EPGY)
Ventura Hall
Stanford University
Stanford, California 94305-4115, 415-723-0512, FAX 415-327-1598

Halbert Robinson Center for the Study of Capable Youth
Guthrie Annex II, NI-20
University of Washington
Seattle,WA 98195, 206-543-4160

Office for Precollegiate Programs for Talented and Gifted
Iowa State University
Ames, IA 50011, 515-294-1772

PULSAR and NOVA Programs
Purdue University
1446 Laeb, Room 5114
West Lafayette, IN 47907-1446, 317-494-7241

Science Summer Institute and Math Talent Development Project
University of Wisconsin-Eau Claire
Arts and Science Department
Eau Claire, WI 54702-4004, 715-836-2031

Wisconsin Center for Academically Talented Youth (WCATY)
2909 Landmark Place
Madison, WI 53713, 608-271-1617

References and Resources

American Association of University Women (1991). *Shortchanging girls, shortchanging America.* Washington DC: American Association of University Women.

Armstrong, T. (1994). *Multiple intelligences in the classroom.* Alexandria, VA: Association for Supervision and Curriculum Development.

Bloom, B., ed. (1985). *Developing talent in young people.* New York: Ballantine Books.

Clark, B. (1992). *Growing up gifted.* New York: Macmillan.

Clasen, R. R., & Clasen, D. R. (1987). *Gifted and talented students: A step-by-step approach to programming.* Madison: Wisconsin Department of Public Instruction.

Cox, J., Daniel, N., & Boston, B. O. (1985). *Educating able learners.* Austin: University of Texas.

Csikszentmihalyi, M., Rathunde, K., & Whalen, S. (1993). *Talented teenagers: The roots of success & failure.* New York: Cambridge University Press.

Daniel, N., & Cox, J., (1988). *Flexible pacing for able learners.* Reston, VA: The Council for Exceptional Children.

Durden, W. G. & Tangherlini, A. E. (1993). *Smart kids: How academic talents are developed and nurtured in America.* Seattle: Hogrefe & Huber.

Engelsgjerd, J. L., Francis, M. K., Miller, M. K., Schuster, N. B., Sorenson, J. S. (1988). *The gifted program handbook.* Palo Alto, CA: Dale Seymour.

Erickson, J. B. (Ed.). (1996). *Directory of American youth organizations.* Minneapolis: Free Spirit.

Feldhusen, J. F. (1990). Unpublished letter.

Feldhusen, J. F. (1995). Challenging the gifted and talented: Acceleration. *Postscript: Newsletter of the Wisconsin Center for Academically Talented Youth,* 4(2).

Gardner, H. (1983). *Frames of mind.* New York: Basic Books.

Guide to summer camps and summer schools. (1995). Boston: Porter Sargent.

Herwig, K. L., & Papp, D. M. (Eds.). (1990). *Advisory list of international educational travel and exchange programs.* Reston, VA: Council on Standards for International Educational Travel.

Kaplan, S. N. (1974). *Providing programs for the gifted and talented: A handbook.* Ventura, CA: Office of the Ventura County Superintendent of Schools.

Marland, S. P. (1972). *Education of the gifted and talented: Report to the Congress of the United States by the U.S. Commissioner of Education.* Washington, DC: Department of Health, Education, and Welfare.

Miller, M. K. (1991). Meeting needs through flexible pacing, pp. 13-19. In Schatz, E. & Jones, E. (Eds.), *At the heart of teaching: A handbook for educators and parents.*

O'Connell Ross, P. (Ed.). (1993). *National excellence — a case for developing America's talent.* Washington, DC: Office of Educational Research and Improvement, U.S. Department of Education.

Olszewski-Kubilius, P. (1989). Development of academic talent: The role of summer programs, pp. 214-230. In Van Tassel-Baska, J. L. & Olszewski-Kubilius, P. (Eds.), *Patterns of influence on gifted learners.* New York: Teachers College Press.

Peters, R. (1994). Working on the puzzle: What to know and do — a sharing of parental thoughts. *Postscript: Newsletter of the Wisconsin Center for Academically Talented Youth,* 3(1).

Reilly, J. M. & Featherstone, B. D. (1987). *College comes sooner than you think!* Hawthorne, NJ: Career Press.

Renzulli, J. S. (1978). What makes giftedness: Reexamining a definition. *Phi Delta Kappan*, 60, 108-184.

Rimm, S. (1990). *How to parent so children will learn.* Watertown, WI: Apple.

Robinson, N. M., & Robinson, H. B. (1982). The optimal match: Devising the best compromise for the highly gifted student, pp. 79-94. In Feldman, D. (Ed.), *New directions for child development: Developmental approaches to giftedness and creativity,* No. 17. San Francisco: Jossey-Bass.

Rogers, K. (1995). [survey of students in the Accelerated Learning Program] Unpublished raw data.

Rolland, A. & Schuster, N. (1988). Wisconsin's mathematics talent development project. *Gifted Child Today,* 11(4), 8-9.

Schatz, E. (1989). Wisconsin's integrated gifted education model. *Education Forward.* Madison: Wisconsin Department of Public Instruction.

Schatz, E. (1991). Dissemination by design - a tool for advancing gifted education. *Gifted Child Quarterly,* 35(4), 188-195.

Schatz, E. (1992). Acceleration across the pyramid. *Understanding Our Gifted,* 5(2), 1, 11-14.

Silverman, L. (1992). Personality plus. *Understanding Our Gifted,* 5(1), 8.

Silverman, L. (Ed.). (1993). *Counseling the gifted & talented.* Denver: Love.

Sorenson, J., Buckmaster, L., Francis, M., & Knauf, K. (1996). *The power of problem solving.* Boston: Allyn and Bacon.

Stanley, J. C. (1976). Identifying and nurturing the intellectually gifted. *Phi Delta Kappan,* 58, 234-237.

Stanley, J. C. (1984). Use of general and specific aptitude measures in identification: Some principles and certain cautions. *Gifted Child Quarterly,* 28(4), 177-180.

Stanley, J. C. (1991). An academic model for educating the mathematically talented. *Gifted Child Quarterly,* 35(1), 36-41.

Stanley, J. C. (1994). Cumulative educational advantage: Devise the positively accelerated trajectory through school and into professional life that is optimal for you. *Postscript: Newsletter of the Wisconsin Center for Academically Talented Youth,* 2(4).

Sykes, C. J. (1995). *Dumbing down our kids: Why America's children feel good about themselves but can't read, write or add.* New York: St. Martin's Press.

Turner, R. & Schwartz, C. A. (Eds.). (1995). *Encyclopedia of associations.* Detroit:Gale Research.

Van Tassel-Baska, J. (1984). The talent search as an identification model. *Gifted Child Quarterly,* 28(4), 172-176.

Walker, S. Y. (1991). *The survival guide for parents of gifted kids.* Minneapolis: Free Spirit.